PLAYING IN THE DIRT & STILL LOVING IT!

---

21 LESSONS FROM MY FATHER'S GARDEN ABOUT GROWTH, HEALING, & CHOOSING TO THRIVE

MARYA PATRICE SHERRON

KI Productions
Noblesville, IN

ISBN:
Softcover 978-1-961605-44-2
Hardcover 978-1-961605-09-1

Library of Congress Control Number: 2024919280

For Maryanne.
Thank you for the spiritual lessons, for your unconditional love,
and for allowing me to sit at your feet until your very last day.

For every woman
who has ever dared
to press her hands into the dirt,
even when life felt barren.

For the ones who plant seeds in faith,
long before the first sprout appears.

For those who have been pruned,
bent by storms,
and yet — still bloom.

For the ones learning that stillness is sacred,
growth is slow,
and beauty often begins beneath the surface.

This garden was created with you in mind.
And it is tended by the same God

who waters your soul
with every sunrise and every quiet rain.

ACKNOWLEDGMENTS
A SPECIAL THANK YOU

One morning in the winter of 2024, I woke up with a question: *If I asked a group of women to go through "Playing in the Dirt & Loving It" — would anyone say yes?* I jumped out of bed and posted my query, "I need six women..."

To my beautiful surprise, eight women responded! Eight women from various parts of the country, and all different ages, beliefs, and seasons of life. I was over-joyed — and proud. I wasn't proud of myself, I was proud of them! Saying "yes" can be difficult, particularly to the unknown.

Our little group connected instantly and for the following four months, we met weekly and talked through the lessons in *Playing in the Dirt.*

> *We laughed.*
> *We cried.*
> *We challenged one another.*
> *We shared our strengths, struggles, and*
> *   weaknesses.*
> *... and we grew.*

Playing in the Dirt grew as well — I owe a huge thank you to the ladies who said *yes* and gave so openly of their time and hearts. I hope you each see your presence in this revision.

PLAYING IN THE DIRT & LOVING IT
THE LADIES GROUP

When women come together and make a commitment to one another and themselves, growth and healing are inevitable.

Marya

"I have been deep in my weeds and have purposely ignored them for years. In navigating *Playing in the Dirt*, I have learned to be present and to take time for myself. With each chapter I found myself "pruning with purpose" rather than continuing to hide within my weeds. My heart is no longer afraid to see the sunlight. I've allowed myself to say *it's time*. Thank you for allowing me to grow and bask in the sun again!"
~ *Angela Sheely Moore*

"*Playing in the Dirt* is a beautiful experience allowing the reader to interactively explore their soul's purpose and passion. By weaving storytelling of heartfelt life experiences with meaningful and thought-provoking quotes connected to the theme of gardening and seasons, Marya takes the reader through a journey of self-discovery that is inspiring and healing. A must-have for anyone looking to dig deeper into their own lives and experience self-growth!"
~ *Sophia Lafayette-Lause, EdD*

"I was in a dry season, praying for more. More depth, more friends, more opportunities with purpose. God's timing is always perfect, when I started reading *Playing in the Dirt and Loving It*, I didn't realize how difficult of a season I was entering. These women, these words, they were the warm hug and encouragement I truly needed. This book really helped me to still my mind, and dig deep within to start my healing journey. Not only that, it has also quenched my thirst and has given me a hunger to continue to grow. I cannot thank Marya enough for bringing us all together, and sparking that fire again."

~ *Melissa Miller*

"I can recall the moment I began journeying through *Playing in the Dirt*. Lying on the sands of Jamaica, this read stirred me to action in a radical way! Beautiful, powerful and purposeful."

~ *Shanell Henry*

"*Playing in the Dirt* was a life changing tool during my divorce. The journal prompts forced me to think, dig deep and reflect. It was easy to read and follow and the journal made me excited for each chapter. Every *lesson* was full of stories that were relatable and gave a wonderful visual to follow. *Playing in the Dirt* was truly healing and helped me re-parent myself in a lot of ways.

~ *Mari Love*

PROLOGUE

I sat on a sheet spread out across the floor of my 400 foot studio on the twenty-third floor in Chicago covered in dirt. The soil was packed underneath my finger nails... and I loved it.

I was only twenty-two
a poor grad student
lonely
broken, but hopeful
...and angry with the choices I had not yet made.

...yet something I would not comprehend for another twenty years was birthed that winter during my season of long-suffering and despair:

Hope.
Growth.
Life.

Not all that is barren will always be so.

CONTENTS

PREFACE

Before you step into these pages, I want to pause and say—I'm so glad you're here.

This book began as a whisper in my soul during a season when I felt buried beneath the weight of life. Not planted. Just buried. Maybe you know what that feels like. Maybe that's where you are right now.

I wrote this for you.

Not the polished version of you. Not the "got it all together" version. But the beautiful, complicated, weary-yet-still-standing version of you—the one who's trying to find meaning in the mess, purpose in the pruning, and hope in the middle of winter.

Playing in the Dirt & Still Loving It is about seasons—both in the garden and in life. You'll find stories of growth, loss, joy, mess-ups, do-overs, and all the tender lessons that bloom when you least expect them. Every story is rooted in something real: my muddy hands, my real-life garden, my mother-heart, my fears, my faith, and the slow, steady work of a God who is always present, even when we feel alone.

You don't need to be a gardener. You don't even have to like dirt. You just need to be open to the idea that your life—yes, yours—is a garden worth cultivating. And that even in the most barren, broken places, God is planting something good.

So come as you are.

Bring your dirt.

Bring your droughts.

Bring your dead ends.

And bring your dreams, too.

Let's play in the dirt together. And let's fall in love with the process.

We begin with winter. Why? It's my most difficult season. I'm a midwest girl born and raised. When I was growing up, power outages, blustery snow storms, icicles as big as my arm, and snow banks that were castles for us kids were the norm in Michigan. As a child, Winter was magical. Her snowflakes and icicles draped from tree-lined streets made the obvious cold easy to over-look.

Now that I'm older I'd much rather take a trip to Whistler when the snow-bug bites. Winter is long and grey. Cold. She makes my body ache and my mind want to slumber. I would love to rediscover Winter's magic...

I struggle with seasonal depression and the gray days of my Indiana home are always tough. Yet, it has been in this season while the grass is dormant and the trees are barren that I learned to value the stillness.

Let's begin.

PART 1

WINTER

1
———

DECIDE

"Every seed planted in faith carries the quiet strength to become a garden."

What if we finished everything we started? I've always marveled at people who seem to glide from start to finish—school papers, fitness routines, DIY projects that actually get D-ed, not just Y'd. Meanwhile, I currently have no less than 37 books in progress (each with a "brilliant" title), a stash of unmailed greeting cards purchased with real emotional intention, and half a home office renovation that began with great Pinterest ambition and ended with a dusty toolbox under my desk.

I've come to accept this about myself—mostly. I get bored easily. I leap from project to project, idea to idea, and I've always needed a little bit of chaos to feel creative. But finishing things? That took time. In fact, it wasn't until I was well into my forties that I began to understand the deep, spiritual significance of finishing what I start. Around my 47th birthday, I received a formal ADHD diagnosis. While it explained a lot of my habits (not all, let's be honest), it didn't explain the ache I carried—the part that medication couldn't touch. I had the passion. I had the tools. But I still felt directionless. Like wandering through a magical forest without a compass, enchanted but perpetually off-course.

Where was I going?

What was I doing?

What was the point?

Turns out, the first seed we plant in any garden—literal or metaphorical—is not action. It's intention. We have to decide. Not halfway. Not when the weather's nice. Not when we're in the mood. Decide.

When I taught college freshmen, I always started our first class with a statistic: "One in four of you will not make it to midterms." Not because I wanted to scare them, but because I wanted them to decide—before the assignments piled up, before real life made an appearance—to finish what they started. I'd walk the aisles of that classroom, looking each student in the eyes and saying, "Decide now. This is going to get hard. And you will want to quit. But finish." The students who took that to heart—the ones who anchored themselves in a deeper reason for being there—were often the ones still in their seats come finals-week.

That reason, *their why,* changed everything. Not the what (a degree, a career), but the why. I still remember one young man telling me he was the first in his family to ever attend college. His why? To build a new path for his younger siblings. Others said they wanted to prove to themselves they were capable, to break generational cycles, to live with purpose. When our why is clear, we're spiritually rooted. We have something to hold onto when the storm hits and the soil gets messy.

So let's start here:

You want to start a small business—why?

You want to run a marathon—why?

You want to write that book—why?

And if your why is rooted in something shallow or shame-driven, that's not failure. That's insight. That's a good place to dig.

Growth doesn't begin with a to-do list. It begins with a decision—the holy kind, the kind whispered in prayer and written in ink on a fresh page. Use your journal today to name the thing you're chasing and then ask your soul the harder question: Why does it matter?

You don't need a 10-year plan or a vision board to begin.

You just need to decide... *because every garden begins as a choice.*

GARDEN BLESSING

May your heart be rooted deep in purpose, and may every seed you plant be watered with holy intention. May your "why" grow strong, even when storms rage around you.

DIRT WORK INVITATION: I DECLARE

CREATE YOUR *DECLARATION TO GROW.*

Find a blank page in your journal or use your Reflection page and title it:

"The Day I Decided"

Now write a short declaration—just for you and God—naming what you're choosing to begin, re-begin, or finish. Don't worry about eloquence. Just be honest.

Here's a simple format to guide you:

"Today, I decide to ... . I commit to tending this with faith and focus. I know it won't be perfect, but I believe it's worth it. This is the beginning of my new beginning."

Sign it. Date it. Maybe even decorate the page with a pressed flower, a doodle, or something meaningful. Return to it when you want to quit. It's your first seed.

Optional Reflection Prompts

What am I deciding today to say yes to?

What have I left half-done out of fear or boredom?

What's one thing I know I need to finish, even if it's imperfect?

PLANT YOUR WHY

What dream or goal has been tugging on your heart?
What is your deep, soul-level reason for wanting it?
What fears rise when you think about committing fully?

Reflection

_____
_____
_____
_____
_____
_____
_____
_____
_____
_____

2

NAME YOUR CIRCLE

"Where two or three are planted together, the harvest is multiplied."

What if the people around us play a critical role in our ability to grow?

I've always wondered why one flower would shrivel up and die while the others nearby thrived. Same garden. Same sun. Same soil. Yet one would wither while its neighbors stood tall and proud. What happened to that one lonely bloom? And how did the others survive?

It took me a while to realize I was asking the same question about myself.

I've never been good at reading instructions. I'd like to say it's a personality quirk, but it's really more of a lifelong pattern. Whether it was a recipe that went sideways or modular furniture that had to be disassembled more than once (okay, four times), I usually thought I could figure it out on my own. That same stubbornness followed me into the garden. For years, I skipped over the plant tags—the ones that gently explain how far apart to space your plants, how much light they need, and how to actually keep them alive.

Eventually, I noticed something consistent on those little tags: many flowering shrubs and perennials recommend planting in groups of three or more. I didn't know why at first, but one summer, something clicked. I knelt down in the cool morning dirt, digging three holes about a foot apart. I nestled a vibrant yellow Canna lily in each one and stood back. As the wind picked up, I watched the thick green leaves stretch and sway, brushing up against each other. They weren't just three plants anymore. They became one graceful, moving, living body.

And just like that, the garden became a metaphor again.

In my mind, those Cannas turned into people. I was reminded of something sacred—something deeply spiritual that I'd heard before but suddenly understood differently:

> "For where two or three gather in my name,
> there am I with them." ~ *Matthew* 18:20

There it was. A biblical blueprint for community. A divine confirmation that we were never meant to grow alone.

That moment sent me back into the house, dirt still on my knees, to search for the verse. And it stayed with me. I thought about the small circle of women in my life who had helped me dig deeper, get real, and keep going when I was tempted to shrivel up like that struggling flower. Friends who prayed when I couldn't form the words. Mentors who reminded me of the vision when I'd lost it. Family members who told me the truth even when it stung.

We are stronger together.

We are steadier when rooted near others.
We are better when we grow in clusters.

Now let me be clear: I'm not saying we should only surround ourselves with people who look, think, and believe like we do. Jesus didn't do that, and I have no intention of doing it either. But I do believe He modeled balance:

1. He had an inner circle—his disciples.
2. He regularly made time to be alone with God.
3. And He lived among people. —*All kinds of people.*

He met them in the middle of their mess, not once they were "ready."

So when I plant now—whether in my garden or in my life—I remember the Cannas. I think about how they flourished when planted together. I think about the strength that comes not from doing it all alone, but from growing side-by-side.

When you think about your circle, who comes to mind?

Who helps you thrive? Who speaks truth into your life? Who prays with you, checks on you, or simply reminds you that you matter?

This isn't about quantity. It's about connection. If you have even one name, you are deeply blessed.

Garden Blessing

❦

May your roots intertwine with kindred souls, and may your spirit dance with those who call you upward. Where two or three are gathered in His name, may you always find strength.

🌱 Dirt Work Invitation: Find Your Circle

ON YOUR REFLECTION page or your journal, draw three overlapping circles like a small cluster of flowers. In each circle, write one name: someone who nourishes you, prays for you, or encourages your growth. These might be mentors, friends, elders, or even a child whose faith inspires you.

No names yet? That's okay. In the center, write the word "Open"—and pray this short prayer:

"Lord, I ask for people who will water my roots. Plant me near those who love You and want to see me grow."

Next, write one thing you can do this week to nurture your circle—send a message, pray for someone, or send an invitation for coffee or a walk. Connection grows with attention.

Reflection

_____

_____

_____

_____

_____

_____

_____

_____

_____

_____

3

─────────

LET GO

"The pruning may feel like loss, but it makes room for the bloom."

What if there are things—or people—in my life that do more harm than good?

I used to wonder what gardeners meant when they said one flower had been "choked out" by another. My imagination would spiral into a dirt-level drama: maybe the flowers were having spats over space, arguing about who had the softest petals, or whispering about who was stealing all the sunlight. I imagined the tulips snubbing the daisies and the lavender being secretly jealous of the roses.

Eventually, I learned the truth. Some plants, often labeled as "enthusiastic" by the overly kind, are really just aggressive invaders. Others come right out and call them what they are— choke weeds. These plants aren't content to bloom quietly. They take over. They strangle. They drain resources from everything around them. What begins as a lovely cluster can quickly become a crowded, tangled mess that leaves little room for anything else to grow.

Each summer, I scroll through local "free plant" listings, and the pattern repeats itself. People offering buckets of day lilies or "spreading ground cover" with the same apologetic captions: "Too much." "Taken over my garden." "Choking everything else out."

That phrase stuck with me: choking everything else out.

It reminded me of something I told my youngest son during our family's water-drinking challenge. He was eleven, full of determination and just the right amount of defiance. He asked if it was possible to drink too much water. I hummed, "Too much of anything is a bad thing," which he met with a doubtful squint. The next day, he was pale and sluggish, with no appetite—an immediate red flag. Dylan always had an appetite. After a few too many urgent trips to the bathroom, he finally confessed: "I drank twelve bottles of water. I thought water was the healthiest thing ever."

"It is, Darling," I said, "but too much of anything is a bad thing."

And I meant it. Fill in the blank with anything—money, solitude, vitamins, likes on social media, time spent with people who drain you—and eventually, too much applies. Even things that are good in moderation become harmful when they overwhelm everything else. A garden can't thrive if one plant steals the space, sunlight, and nutrients. And neither can we.

Balance will always reign. Spiritual weeding is growth.

Unlike our internal growth, flower beds are easier to thin out. You'll still need some elbow grease and a sharp tool to separate thick roots, but once you've done the work, everything breathes again. The beauty returns. The blooms have room to stretch. That's the kind of freedom we forget we need.

So now it's your turn to take inventory.

What needs to be thinned out in your life? Maybe even completely uprooted? Think of it like walking through the doors of your home:

What doors need to be closed for good?
What needs to be placed on the curb with a "Free" sign?
What belongs in a garage sale of your past?
What should be given away, no strings attached?
What needs to be burned—cleansed by holy fire so it no longer has power over you?

It doesn't matter how you release it. What matters is that you do. Because anything—*anything*—that chokes out your joy, your peace, or your God-given growth doesn't deserve space in your garden.

I'll go first:

→ *I have a few relationships that are no longer healthy to maintain.*
→ *I have a few mindsets that need to be set out (starting with the unrealistic expectations I place on others).*
→ *And I still need to examine my inability to say no. It's sneaky. It always comes back dressed as kindness.*

Use your Reflection page to make your own list. Be bold. Be honest. Take a good look at what stands out. What's been choking you for far too long?

Maybe it's time to make space for something better to grow.

THINNING THE GARDEN:

⋯→ *What is crowding or choking your ability to grow right now?*

⋯▸ *Name at least one habit, relationship, or mindset that you feel prompted to prune or remove.*

⋯▸ *Pray for wisdom and courage to create space for healthy growth.*

Garden Blessing
⚓

May you have the courage to pull every weed with bold hands, and may your soil be made clear and clean, ready to nurture only what God has planted within you.

🌿 Dirt Work Invitation: The Garden Clean-out

DRAW a simple front door on a blank page—or use one of your choosing. Now imagine your life as the house behind that door. Around the steps and the lawn, things have accumulated. Some need to go.

Let's Start Sorting

⋯▸ *What needs to be shut out (habits, noise, toxic cycles)?*

⋯▸ *What needs to be given away (resentment, expectations, comparison)?*

⋯▸ *What needs to be burned (shame, lies, unforgiveness)?*

⋯→ *What needs to be sold at a garage sale (old roles, labels, or identities that no longer fit)?*

Choose just one item from your list and write this over it:

"I release this so something new can grow."

Then close with a prayer: *"God, give me the strength to clear what's choking me. Let Your truth rise where weeds once grew."*

Reflection

_____
_____
_____
_____
_____
_____
_____
_____
_____
_____

4

BE A VISIONARY

"The Master Gardener gave you a license to create—
no fences, no fear."

What if the world lost all of its visionaries?

I've always been curious about what makes some people creative and freely empowered to imagine, take risks, and color outside the lines. Those fearless in spirit who don't seem to care what others think. I admire them deeply. Perhaps everyone is creative, but only some walk boldly in their gifting — and when they do, they change the world. Having kept my creative impulses and limitless imagination bottled up for over forty years, I am deeply passionate about the necessity to express the beauty planted in our minds and hearts.

I was raiseed to color in the lines, follow all the rules, and to read instructions multiple times (*more on this later*). Little room was left for the creative impulses of a child. But as our Lord so often does, he sent a messenger to plant a seed.

I remember it so clearly. I was in second grade and we had

art class once a week with Miss Lou. We always looked forward to her visits and we never understood why we had to do reading and arithmetic every day, but art was only once a week.

It started like any other class: a piece of construction paper, a palette of tempera paints, and the distinct smell of glue mingled in the air. Miss Lou, with her calming voice and linen smock, strolled table to table, handing each of us a long-stemmed flower.

"Now," she said, demonstrating at the front of the room, "I want you to dip your flower in one color and press it on your paper. Do this a few times, then trade flowers with a friend."

And just like that, the classroom erupted in color and chaos. Children were dipping, pressing, dragging, and flinging paint with unbridled joy. I, on the other hand, froze. After my first few stamps, I panicked. I didn't know what came next. I stared at Miss Lou's sample sheet, waiting for further instruction. But she had moved on, overseeing the joy in motion.

My face flushed hot. My eyes welled with tears. I didn't want to mess it up. *I didn't want to do it wrong.*

That's when everything slowed down. I noticed the girl next to me was only using one color, clearly breaking the rules — Miss Lou only used one color. And to my utter shock, Miss Lou peered over her shoulder and said, "Oh, how nice. You've chosen a polychromatic theme. Well done!"

Wait, what? Not only was it okay, it was celebrated?

I finally let my tears spill. "I don't know what you want me to do next," I told Miss Lou, trying to steady my voice. "You didn't finish your example and I just want mine to be right."

Her expression softened with a knowing smile. "Oh, dear," she said. "You've missed the point of art, Marya."

Then she did something I'll never forget. She walked to the front, grabbed a sheet of green construction paper, and began cutting it into small squares. "I have something very special to give each of you today," she said, "but you must promise never to lose it."

We looked on with curiosity and awe as she passed a square to each child.

"This," she said, holding one up high, "is your Creative License. It's your license to be creative. *You are free to create. Free to be imaginative. Free to see things in new ways.* There is no right way—which also means," she added, looking straight at me, "there isn't a wrong way when it comes to your creativity and your imagination."

THAT MOMENT TATTOOED itself on my soul. Her eyes saw me—really saw me. That green paper square became a holy relic in my life. It was my very own Creative License.

At first, it was a bit too much power for a second grader to handle. I stopped folding the laundry the way Mama liked. I reimagined when dessert should be served (immediately after lunch made far more sense). I even redesigned our table setting, placing all the utensils on the right since we were all right-handed. I was bursting with newly licensed brilliance.

My family, however, was less than thrilled. Mama scolded me about the "proper" way to fold clothes and insisted that my ideas about the silverware were "just wrong." I secretly think everyone enjoyed dessert after lunch, but tradition won out. The "right way" was the only way.

And I wondered... had my parents lost their Creative License? Or worse, had they never been given one?

As I grew older, my creativity matured. I couldn't sing like Mama or dance and act like my brother, but my imagination became my gift—my truest strength. It's the place where God first met me, the place where I felt free. And how fitting that He would use a flower to teach me that.

. . .

WHAT I'VE since realized is this: there are many adults who have misplaced or never received their Creative License. These are the folks who say, "We've always done it this way." They cling to outdated beliefs, rigid roles, and unnecessary rules without stopping to ask if those things still serve anyone. *There is no greater sign of lost vision than the refusal to imagine something new.*

A visionary is defined as someone who plans and sees the future with imagination and wisdom. Synonyms include: *inventive, imaginative, insightful, inspired.*

Doesn't that sound like someone we need more of?

So let me ask: How will you use your Creative License?

Use the Reflection page to explore your own imaginative energy. What ideas have you tucked away? What visions are waiting to be shared? What corners of the world could be better if you dared to imagine a new way?

You have visions and creative impulses that no one else has. And yes, they matter.

Share them. Steward them. Use them well.

Garden Blessing

❦

May your creativity bloom wild and untamed, unbound by fear, tradition, or expectation. You are licensed to dream — and to dream boldly.

🌱 DIRT WORK INVITATION: RECLAIM YOUR LICENSE

TAKE A GREEN PIECE OF PAPER—OR draw a small green square in your journal. Label it boldly:

"My Creative License"

NOW, answer these reflection prompts around or inside your square:

🌷 *What creative things did I love as a child?*

🌷 *When did I start believing there was a "right" way?*

🌷 *Where in my life do I still hide or hesitate out of fear of doing it "wrong"?*

Under your answers, write:

"There is no wrong way to create."

Decorate your Creative License however you like. Tape it to your mirror, tuck it in your Bible, or keep it in your journal. Then choose one small, bold act of creative expression this week—write a poem, wear colors that make you feel alive, rearrange your furniture, or cook something wild. This is your permission slip to be you.

Optional Reflection Prompts

> ❀ *What dreams or ideas have you put on hold because you feared doing them "wrong"?*

> ❀ *What creative gift has God planted uniquely inside of you?*

> ❀ *Write a Creative Declaration: "I will create because..."*

A visionary is: adjective. (especially of a person) thinking about or planning the future with imagination or wisdom.

. . .

SYNONYMS: *inventive, imaginative, ingenious, insightful, inspired*

How will you use your Creative License?

Reflection

5

YOU ARE WORTH THE WAIT

"Time is the soil where tomorrow's beauty takes root."

What if we valued our time the same way we value our money —or our favorite belongings? I always wondered about the mysteries of time.

Time is simply fascinating. Elusive. *Sacred.* In some ways, it's the only true currency we have, yet we often toss it around like loose change in the bottom of an old purse.

Time is a great mystery I long to understand. I want to dance with time. How does it bend, stretch, contract? How can something so ordinary also be so divine?

"With the Lord a day is like a thousand years, and a thousand years are like a day." ∼ *2 Peter* 3:8

That verse never fails to stop me in my tracks. One day... like a thousand years. My mind can't quite wrap around it.

God, the creator of the universe we know, the One who
sculpted time itself, doesn't even operate on our clock. And yet,
we try to manage it—measure it, control it, race against it.

"As I looked, thrones were set in place, and the Ancient of Days
took his seat." ~ *Daniel 7:9*

I love that name: *Ancient of Days*. He who was, and is,
and is to come. He who made the sun stand still and who
holds every hour of our lives in His hands. He created time.
He separated night from day and marked seasons with stars.
His Son's birth and resurrection reset the calendar for the
entire world. And yet... we treat our minutes like they're
disposable.

Seconds slip by like pennies. We think they're too small to
matter—until we look back and realize they added up to a life.

ONE OF THE few quotes I memorized as a child was from
Benjamin Franklin:

"Do not squander time, for it is the stuff life is made of."

I didn't fully understand it then, but something about those
words stuck. I was the kid always thinking about what was next
—next birthday, next grade, next Saturday morning cartoon.
Time felt slow, painfully slow, especially when you're always
looking forward. I didn't yet know that time speeds up the
moment you learn to appreciate it.

To this day, patience is not my strong suit. I have to work at
being present, at staying where my body is instead of letting my
mind run three miles, three days, or three years ahead. Slowing

down doesn't come naturally to me. But the older I get, the more I'm convinced: God's timing is perfect.

I was reminded of this when my oldest son was little. Any time I said, "Not now," or "I'll think about it," he heard one thing:

No.

I meant it sincerely when I said, "I'll think about it," — I was going to consider it. I needed a moment. But to him, "Not now" felt like the end of the road. So he stopped asking. Eventually, he stopped dreaming out loud. I couldn't help but wonder if I had ever done the same thing. Had I stopped going to God? Stopped sharing the longings of my heart? Stopped praying and communing with him when my requests were not answered?

Observing my son's withdrawal pierced me. I had to learn that even my language around time had power. *A pause doesn't mean denial. A delay isn't rejection.* I started to be more careful with how I answered him—because time, especially a child's sense of it, is tender ground. It can plant trust or sow doubt. It can nurture hope or steal it before it ever takes root.

In many ways, we're just like him. When God says, "Wait," we hear, "No."

When He says, "Not yet," we brace ourselves for disappointment.

We'd rather hear a firm "Yes" or a clean "No," not the uncomfortable silence in between.

But this is the truth I now Know: *some of the holiest things in life grow during that sacred silence.*

TIME IS both fast and slow. It matures our minds and ages our bodies. It builds families and breaks routines. It makes us treasure what we once took for granted. And while we may never fully understand its dimensions, we can choose to honor it.

What are you doing with the time you've been given?
Are you spending it or squandering it?
Are you racing it or reverencing it?

Remember: you can't control the clock. But you can choose how you move within it.

And that choice—that posture of surrender—is one of the most powerful ways to worship the One who created it.

GARDEN BLESSING

☥

May you savor the sacredness of each second, knowing that time is a gift, not a guarantee. May you live fully rooted in each holy moment.

🌱 DIRT WORK INVITATION: TENDING TIME

DRAW A CLOCK FACE ON A PAGE—NO numbers, just a circle with a small center point. Around the outside, write:

Things that give me energy
Things that drain my energy
Things I wish I had more time for
Places I waste time without noticing

Now draw small "roots" coming from the center of the clock. Label the center:

God's Timing

Along one root, write this Scripture:

"With the Lord a day is like a thousand years..."
~ 2 Peter 3:8

Then write:

"I want to spend my time like it's holy.
Lord, show me where to pause and where to grow."

If time has been a thief in your life—robbing you with distractions or regret—take one moment to reclaim it. Circle one area from the clock where you want to be more intentional this week. Let that be your first new seed.

See Time as Sacred

···▸ *What is one way you can slow down and savor the time you are given today?*

···▸ *Are there areas where impatience has robbed you of peace?*

Write a prayer asking the Lord to help you see time through His eyes.

Reflection

_____
_____
_____
_____
_____
_____
_____
_____
_____
_____
_____
_____

PART 2

SPRING

6

KEEP YOUR HEAD ABOVE WATER

"Water wisely; not every thirst leads to life."

I've always wondered about the fine line that separates our strengths from our weaknesses.

What if I create many of the obstacles I face — or my own choices and habits are worst enemy?

I've always been fascinated by the fine, blurry line between our strengths and our weaknesses—how something that once helped us survive can later become the very thing that holds us back. How the same pattern that comforted us in one season might smother us in another. It's a wild thought, but here's the kicker: what if the thing we reach for to grow... is the very thing slowly drowning us?

You made it through the long winter. I know winter doesn't drag on for everyone, but for those of us who struggle— mentally, emotionally, spiritually—it can feel eternal. But then spring arrives, and the world shifts. Crocuses poke their way through the soil like tiny prophets. Daffodils and tulips stretch their necks toward the sun. Trees bud with a quiet promise.

Even the grass seems to exhale, shaking off its brittle yellow coat in exchange for green.

Spring is a time of renewal. A time to grow. A time to come back to life.

But spring, as lovely as it is, doesn't work without one essential ingredient: *water*. Spring simply cannot be what it is or do what it does without it!. Water is vital to our existence, both literally and spiritually. Arguably, we cannot survive beyond a handful of days without water. I'm ashamed to admit that I have lived the bulk of my life completely dehydrated — I mean days upon days without water. Ironically, when it comes to my garden and plants, if they did not survive it was more likely than not because I watered the poor things to death.

> *Not growing* — must need water!
> *Yellow leaves* — must need water!
> *Not blooming* — must need water!
> *Brown leaves* — must need water!

Looking back, maybe I was subconsciously projecting my own dryness onto them. Either way, water was always the answer... until it wasn't.

Plain and simple, I drowned them.

My *planticide** was cause to pause and try to figure out what I was doing wrong. "Yep, you got root rot," my neighbor sighed after examining a few of my indoor potted plants. "Gnats aren't far behind." Root rot! Gnats! The process of repotting and in some cases, washing the roots and starting over with fresh dirt was tedious, but examining the roots was fascinating. The task itself allowed me to sit with them long enough to learn how to help them thrive. Some roots were thick and

---

* *Maryaism -- Creative License Approved*

unbreakable while others were soft and fine like thread. It was easy to see the effect too much water had on them.

Eventually, I had to face the truth: my plants weren't thirsty—they were drowning.

"Yep, you've got root rot," my neighbor sighed after examining a few of my pitiful indoor pots. "Gnats aren't far behind."

Root rot. Gnats. My garden had become a cautionary tale. I had to dig them out, wash their roots, repot them with fresh soil. It was tedious. It was messy. But also? It was kind of miraculous. Sitting with those plants, studying their roots—some thick and strong, others soft and threadbare—I realized how telling roots can be. They always tell the truth. They don't lie about what's been happening underground.

And then it hit me. *I knew what drowning felt like.*

THE THOUGHT of drowning was all too familiar (and unwelcome) for me. Past seasons of life submerged in water floated by like seaweed...

> *Drowning in grief.*
> *Drowning in anger.*
> *Drowning in pride.*
> *Drowning in singleness.*
> *Drowning in marriage.*
> *Drowning in debt.*
> *Drowning in abundance.*
> *Drowning in bad choices.*
> *Drowning in guilt.*
> *... simply drowning*

—and all the while, being utterly parched.

Internally, I was as dry as the desert. Externally, I was treading the wrong waters—standing in floods I had no business being in. I needed a reset. A rebalancing. A reckoning with what I had allowed to flood my life.

It was time to strike a healthy balance with water—in my soil, in my body, in my spirit.

Take a few minutes to think about your current conditions. Are you drowning or parched? Or both? What does water symbolize in this season in life? Pray. Ask our Lord to show you where you are and what surrounds you. Ask Him for the coming of the spring rains that will produce life, not decay or rot.

"For as the soil makes the sprout come up and a garden causes seeds to grow, so the Sovereign Lord will make righteousness and praise spring up before all nations." ~ *Isaiah 61:11*

Use your Reflection page to name the areas in your life where you may be drowning. Go deep. Don't stop at surface-level stressors. Sit with the hard questions and listen for the root.

I'll start:

I'm drowning in concern for my parents as they age.
I'm drowning in my ability to keep up.
I'm drowning in missing my youth.
Will I finish my dream project in time?
Will it even matter to anyone?
Am I the problem in our marriage?
Is there a problem to begin with?
Will my boys be okay?

... and on and on it goes.

· · ·

THERE'S TOO much water around me, and not enough within me.

Could it be that my internal (spiritual) fears are leaking into my external life? That my lack of confidence is showing up in how I relate to others? Maybe I'm not broken—maybe I'm just overwatered. Maybe I need to drain some old habits before I can enter a new season of growth.

This is how we go deep. We don't just prune the leaves —*we check the roots*. We ask honest questions. And we sit long enough with the mess to hear something that will actually help us grow.

Garden Blessing

May living water fill you where the droughts have left you barren, and may the floods recede, leaving behind fertile, ready soil. May you drink deeply of His life-giving Spirit.

Dirt Work Invitation: Water Check

DRAW two side-by-side jars (or use two jars). Label one *"Drowning"* and the other *"Parched."*

Inside the Drowning jar, list the areas of your life that feel overwhelming right now. What are you submerged in? *Fear? Guilt? Debt? Expectations?*

In the Parched jar, list the areas that feel dry. Where are

you longing for nourishment? *Your spirit? Marriage? Friend-ships? Energy?*

Beneath your jars, draw a small watering can and write this prayer:

"Lord, pour Living Water into what is dry in me, and teach me where to stop the flood. Let me thirst for You above all else."

Then choose one thing to remove from the "Drowning" list this week (a task, a thought, a toxic pattern), and one thing to replenish from the "Parched" list (Scripture, sunlight, laughter, sleep, grace).

Keep your jars somewhere visible. Let this be your reminder: *balance is holy work.*

Optional Reflection Prompts

Overwatering or Parched:

⇨ *Are you overwatering or undernourishing any area of your life?*

⇨ *Where do you sense root rot — or thirst — in your spirit?*

⇨ *Write a prayer asking the Lord to balance your soul with His perfect provision.*

Reflection

_____
_____
_____
_____
_____
_____
_____
_____
_____
_____

7

CHECK YOUR DIRT

*"Rich soil is not a luxury; it is the quiet work
beneath every bloom."*

What if something seemingly simple in our environment is
quietly hindering our growth?

I've always been fascinated by the ordinary things we over-
look—the subtle stuff in our environment that shapes us, molds
us, and sometimes even stunts us. Case in point: red dirt.

In the late '90s, feeling a little grown, a little wild, and just
free enough to book a cheap flight, I headed down to Atlanta to
visit my best friend from high school. Having grown up in the
Midwest, I was struck by how alive the South felt. It was a
sensory experience—the air thick with fragrance, the flowers
unapologetically bold, the leaves glossier, the greens greener.
But it was the dirt that stopped me.

It wasn't brown. It wasn't dusty. It was red. More specifi-
cally, rust-colored. I reached down to touch it, expecting

powder or sand. But it was dense—almost like clay. Heavy. Tangible. Strange.

Years later, my vintage gardening book helped me understand what I was seeing. The color of soil, it turns out, comes from the minerals in it. That iconic red Georgia clay is packed with iron oxide—hematite, to be exact. And the presence (or lack) of other minerals, along with water and temperature, all impact how soil behaves. I also learned that soil oversaturated with water loses its oxygen. (Which confirmed, once again, that I was not just drowning my plants—I was smothering them.)

Let me be plain:

If your dirt isn't right, nothing will grow.

That truth smacked me in the face. It also brought to mind a moment in Scripture I'd always found haunting:

> "The next day as they were leaving Bethany, Jesus was
> hungry. Seeing in the distance a fig tree in leaf, he went
> to find out if it had any fruit. When he reached it, he
> found nothing but leaves." ~ *Mark* 11:12-13

It had leaves, y'all. It looked healthy. It gave the appearance of life. But it wasn't bearing anything. No fruit. Nothing nourishing. Nothing to show for its existence.

I've been there. Haven't you?

Walking around full of leafy busyness, saying yes to things, showing up in life, but inwardly... dry. Stunted. Disconnected from what matters. Bearing no fruit. But, why?

> Could it have been the quality of the dirt?
> Can we be alive/living and yet produce no
>   fruit?

Later, Jesus will say:

"I am the vine; you are the branches. If you remain in me
and I in you, you will bear much fruit; apart from me
you can do nothing. If you do not remain in me, you
are like a branch that is thrown away and withers;
such branches are picked up,
thrown into the fire and burned.
If you remain in me and my words remain in you,
ask whatever you wish, and it will be done for you.
This is to my Father's glory,
that you bear much fruit,
showing yourselves to be my disciples." ~ *John 15:5-8*

The soil that sustains us spiritually must be balanced. Not perfect. Not identical to anyone else's. But balanced. If one component is too much—or another too little—it disrupts the whole system. We might look okay on the outside, but if our roots are gasping for air or starving for nutrients, we will not thrive. We might survive. But fruit? Not likely.

So today, we're not just looking at what's around us. We're getting real about what's feeding us.

Our dirt is made up of the quiet choices, the unnoticed habits, the influences we allow in without even thinking. And not everything in your dirt is "bad." That's the tricky part. Some things are good—until they're not.

Here's a simple example from my life: news consumption.

The good: I want to be informed. I care about my community, my country, and this messy, beautiful world. Staying engaged is a form of responsibility.

The not-so-good: Too much news—especially biased, fear-driven, 24/7 coverage—affects my mood, my thoughts, and how I feel about people. It slowly poisons my soil.

· · ·

SO NOW I have to ask myself:
What are the ingredients in my dirt?
How much am I taking in?
From where is it coming?
How does it leave me feeling?

IF THE ANSWERS point toward imbalance? Then I need to be ready to adjust. Immediately.
So let me ask you:
What's in your soil these days?
Are you spiritually oversaturated? Emotionally depleted?
Is there something that looks harmless—but is quietly taking up too much space?

SOMETIMES, it's not what we're doing that's wrong — it's the invisible conditions around us. Dirt matters. We must regularly check our dirt.

Garden Blessing

⚘

May your soil be rich with truth, and may your roots stretch deep into holy ground. May you bear fruit in season, and may your leaves never wither.

🌱 Dirt Work Invitation: Soil Sample

DRAW A GARDEN BED. In each corner, write one major area of your life—examples:

Relationships, Faith, Work, Mindset (or choose your own).

Now assess the soil of each area. Next to each one, answer:

Is the soil rich or poor?

Am I feeding it with truth, grace, or something else entirely?

Has something made the soil toxic?

Do I need to add nutrients, or just pull some weeds?

LABEL THE WHOLE PAGE:

"Lord, test my soil."

Then circle the one area that needs the most care. Write this underneath:

"Father, show me how to enrich this soil. I want to bear good fruit."

This week, commit to adding one spiritual or emotional nutrient to that area—maybe less screen time, a walk, forgiveness, journaling, or prayer. Dirt can change. It just needs tending.

Reflection

_____
_____
_____
_____
_____
_____
_____
_____
_____
_____

8

"DORMANT" IS NOT "DEAD"

"What looks barren may yet be bursting with unseen life."

What if life still lingers in what we've already given up for dead?

I've always been curious about the way some things surprise us by refusing to quit. Take my flowers, for instance. I've planted plenty of "annuals" in my garden—those supposedly one-and-done blooms that, by all Midwestern standards, shouldn't return once the frost has had its way. And yet... year after year, my so-called annuals come back. Stronger. Fuller. Determined.

We're talking about Indiana here—Zone 5—where the winters don't play around. Freezing temperatures. Snow. Ice. Sleet. The works. By all logic, my elephant ears and pansies should be long gone. But somehow, they rise again.

The first year I planted elephant ears, I dutifully dug them up at the end of the season and stored the root balls in my garage, wrapped and waiting. The following year? I forgot. Completely. Left them in the ground like a rookie. Imagine my surprise when, by mid-summer, those beautiful, broad leaves came bursting up from the soil like they had something to prove.

How? I'm not entirely sure. I'll leave the science to someone with more official credentials. I'm a self-taught gardener—I do what works and don't repeat what didn't. What I can tell you is this: for over a decade, I've left my elephant ears in the ground, and they show up faithfully every summer. Maybe it's one thing, maybe it's all of the below:

1. *I bury my elephant ears deep — so deep, the rain does not mushify* the root ball.*
2. *I buy a few bags of mulch every fall and pour them over my beds, as well as rake my leaves over them. Everything is coated and cozy for the long winter.*
3. *My beds are in well-drained locations.*

Whatever the case, those roots stay tucked in through winter. Dormant. Not dead.

And my pansies? I've got a whole row dedicated just for them. When summer rolls in, I plant heat-loving petunias in front of them so the pansies get some shade and protection. I've seen gardeners yank up perfectly healthy pansies to make room for flashier plants. Why? Because they assume the pansies are about to die. But sometimes? They're not. Sometimes they just need a little help. A little patience. A little cover.

And here's where it hit me:

---

* *Maryaism ... isn't mushified a great word!? Say a few times out loud... you'll love it!*

We do this to ourselves.
We do this to each other.
We confuse dormant with dead.
We mistake stillness for failure.
We rip out parts of our lives that were only resting.

I've learned to leave things in the dirt a little longer. To pause before pulling up what might still be preparing for its return. Because God designed us with resilience. He hardwired our spirits to survive. Like roots stretching sideways for water, we were built to find a way. And sometimes, what looks like the end is just a season of deep, quiet, unseen preparation.

Let's talk popular culture for a minute.

I remember a commercial years ago (for a cable company, of all things) that made fun of our "cancel-and-replace" mindset:

"Wife not working... *get a new one!*" was the line that grabbed me.

It was meant to be funny. And it was. But — it wasn't because of the underlying truth within the statement.

We've become too quick to toss.

Too quick to replace.

Too quick to assume something—or someone—is finished.

We see the shiny, newer version and get swept up in the lie that newer always means better. But sometimes? Newer just means unproven. And what we needed all along was already right there—waiting to rise again.

So let me ask:

Have you ever thrown something away—something mean-ingful—only to realize it just needed time?

A relationship? A calling? A piece of yourself?

Have you labeled something "dead" that was actually just dormant?

. . .

WHAT ABOUT A DREAM? A goal? A God-seed planted deep within your spirit that once made your heart race? Did you abandon it when it got hard, when the results didn't come quickly, or when fear whispered that you weren't good enough?

Let me tell you something, in case no one else has lately:

'Not yet' is not the same as 'no.'

'Dormant' is not the same as 'dead.'

And dusting off your dreams isn't silly—it's faith.

If you're not sure where to start, take just one step. Ask someone who's done what you want to do. Say it out loud. Write it down. Call it back to life.

Maybe now isn't the season to launch, but it could be the season to prepare. Start tilling the soil. Lay the groundwork. Study. Save. Pray. Heal. Stretch your roots. Whatever you do, don't give up on something just because it's not blooming yet.

> "There is a time for everything,
> and a season for every activity under the heavens."
> ~ *Ecclesiastes* 3:1

GARDEN BLESSING
✿

May you trust the seeds hidden beneath the cold earth, and may you believe in resurrection even when all seems barren. Life stirs in unseen places.

🌱 DIRT WORK INVITATION: STILL ROOTED

FOLD a journal page in half vertically. On one side, title it:

"What I Thought Was Dead"

On the other:

"What Might Just Be Dormant"

Now, begin listing.

ON THE DEAD SIDE, name old dreams, friendships, parts of yourself you've buried, or situations you've given up on.

Then pause.

LOOK at each one and ask:

"Was it truly dead, or was it simply not yet time?"

Move any items you feel a tug of hope for to the dormant side. Beneath this column, write:

"I give these dreams room to breathe and time to bloom. I trust Your timing, Lord."

Optional: circle one dormant thing and write a gentle action step to tend it (even just praying over it).

You don't have to replant everything. But let nothing be uprooted before its season.

Reflection

_____

_____

_____

_____

_____

_____

_____

_____

_____

_____

9

EMBRACE YOUR FACETS

"You are not one thing. You are a garden full of wild and wondrous blooms."

What if the labels we've been given—or the ones we chase—are actually doing more harm than good?

I've always been a little bewildered by the question: "What are you?" Not who, but what. It's usually asked just after meeting me. The tone is casual, but the subtext is anything but. As a multi-racial woman with seasonally fair skin, freckles, angular features, and curly hair, I've never fit neatly into any of the pre-set racial boxes American culture seems to prefer. The question is about my race. Always has been.

Over the years, I've answered it in different ways—depending on my mood, the environment, the current racial climate, or the latest national headline. I too have been curious about people's backgrounds, but here's the difference: what I'm most curious about is *who* they are. Not what category they belong to. Not what demographic data they fulfill. *But who.*

It's so much easier to file someone away into a box than to do the deeper work of discovering their heart.

One of my favorite stories came from my dad—"Smitty"—who worked for the Michigan Department of Transportation back in the day. Dad never met a stranger. He was the kind of guy who made friends with security guards and janitors because, in his eyes, everyone deserved to be seen.

One day, Dad was coming back from lunch and pulled the glass door open. He noticed that two security guards who he talked with often were mumbling when one hesitantly shot out,

> "Yo, Smitty... is it true? *You married to a white woman?*"

Dad stopped in his tracks and looked up in careful contemplation before answering,

> "... *I don't know... I never asked her.*"

That moment is one I treasure. It said more than the clever words themselves. It revealed a way of seeing people that didn't begin and end with skin. He was saying: I married her. I chose her. We raised two children. We survived loss and loved through grief. We shared laughter, built a life, dreamed dreams. The least important thing about her was the color of her skin. I will never forget this. Ever.

LET ME PAUSE HERE. I'm not suggesting we erase or ignore our rich cultures or our ethnicity. I believe in the beauty of culture, the power of heritage, and the deep knowing that comes from honoring our histories. I don't support the "I don't see color" narrative—because I do see color, and it matters. But

I also believe in what my father was expressing: that love can choose to prioritize relationship over labels. That curiosity about someone's identity should go deeper than a singular category.

For me, the most transformative shifts in identity came not from racial identity, but from becoming a wife and a mother. Both roles stretched and reshaped me in ways I couldn't have predicted. And the deeper I went into those callings, the more I realized: we are layered. Identity is not one thing. It is many things, lived simultaneously and changing constantly.

I began to think of myself as a faceted gemstone.

In gemology, facets are the flat, angled surfaces cut into transparent stones. Each one is designed to reflect light—to give the stone brilliance and clarity. The more precise the cut, the more it sparkles.

Here are just a few of my facets:

> *I am a Mother (a boy-mom).*
> *I am a Wife.*
> *I am a Daughter.*
> *I am a Sister.*
> *I am a Disciple of Jesus Christ.*
> *I am a Storyteller.*
> *I am a culturally Black, multi-racial woman.*
> *... and I am a Gardener— a* Storyteller of
> Nature.

And when it comes to my work?
I've been a teacher.
A collegiate professor.
A secondary administrator.
A small business owner.
A publisher.

An author.

A screenwriter.

A public speaker.

An autism advocate and ally.

A director and documentarian.

And the truth is, I'm still doing most of those things. Is it necessary to do just one thing? To be just one thing? I say no. I say it's not only unnecessary—it's unnatural.

We are richly woven—layered tapestries with threads that shimmer and stretch. We are not made to be confined. We are not built for boxes.

We are multifaceted, radiant gemstones—each angle a story, each edge a survival, each plane reflecting the light of the One who made us.

My beautiful, melodious mother named me after an old country song, They Call the Wind Mariah. She used to sing it to me every night, her voice soft and steady, like the wind itself. I adored that song. Not just for the tune, but for the mystery of the lyrics. I was young, and the idea that the wind could be named felt like magic.

And though my spelling is a bit different—Marya—I've always loved the sound of it. Pre-Mariah Carey, it was uncommon, whimsical, original. I've been called many things in my life—each name carrying its own kind of wind. And the older I get, the more I appreciate the sacredness of being known by the One who named me first.

So, who am I?

I am Marya.

I am a daughter of the one true King.

I am a follower of Christ, a friend of God, and an heir with Jesus.

I am a future crown-bearer and mansion resident.

I am an image-bearer.

I am the reason for the cross.

I am God's why, Jesus' yes, and the Holy Spirit's home.

I am Marya.

I am many things — but most of all, I am His.

...And so are you.

GARDEN BLESSING

⚓

May you shine with the brilliance of all your many God-crafted facets. May you wear your names, your roles, and your stories like precious jewels, reflecting His light into the world.

DIRT WORK INVITATION: FACETS OF ME

DRAW A LARGE, imperfect gemstone on the page. Give it playful cuts, odd angles, asymmetry—just like real life. Label the center:

I am God's Masterpiece

In each facet of your gem, name a truth about who you are —not what you do or who you are to others, but who you are in Christ and who you are becoming.

Some prompts to consider:

What do I love deeply?

What strengths do I carry?

What makes me me?

What has God whispered about me that the world doesn't always see?

. . .

EXAMPLES:

    I am curious.

    I am resilient.

    I am tenderhearted.

    I am whole even when healing.

    I am an image-bearer of the Divine.

    Around the outside of the gem, write:

"I am multifaceted. I am not just one thing. I am loved and chosen in every form I take."

READ YOUR WORDS ALOUD. Let them root. You are not solely someone's daughter, wife, or titleholder. You are God's handcrafted brilliance.

Reflection

_____
_____
_____
_____
_____
_____
_____
_____
_____
_____

10

LEARN THE MIGHTY OAK

"The deeper the root, the stronger the storm's surrender."

What if the most important part of the flower or plant or tree is what we don't see — the roots?

I always wondered how deep roots really go and what makes them thrive.

I'm reminded of a sermon about our spiritual roots:

The stronger your roots, the stronger your trunk — and the better you can weather the storms.

What if the most important part of the flower—or plant, or tree—is the part we never see?

I've always been curious about roots. How far do they stretch? What makes them thrive? What holds a tree upright through the seasons, year after year, storm after storm?

One Sunday morning, I heard a powerful sermon that flipped something inside of me. The pastor said, "If your roots are deep, your trunk will stand." That's it. That's the sermon.

Of course, there was more, but that line stuck. If our roots are healthy—spiritually, emotionally, relationally—we become grounded, anchored, unshakable. The winds will blow. The seasons will change. But we won't fall.

Let's talk about plants for a second. Healthy roots are a plant's secret strength. They do the invisible, essential work. Roots keep the plant steady. They reach deep to pull up water and nutrients. They store energy for growth when the time is right. Roots feed everything above the surface. But they don't just exist for survival. They're made for thriving.

For a root system to flourish, it needs three things:

1. Water – the kind that nourishes from the inside out
2. Oxygen – space to breathe, rest, and stretch
3. Nutrient-rich soil – dirt that holds substance, not just show

It's a beautiful metaphor, isn't it?
Your dirt feeds your roots.
Your roots feed everything else.
But even in the best soil, storms still come. Droughts happen. Disease shows up. And the most majestic tree can still wither from the bottom up if its root system isn't strong.

So what about the mighty oak? Why does it stand tall when others bend and break?

Oak trees have something special: *a taproot.* A single, bold root that grows straight down from the trunk—deep into the earth. It serves as an anchor. While other roots spread wide, the taproot goes deep. It doesn't shout for attention. It doesn't wave in the wind. But it holds everything in place.

Only about 5% of trees have taproots. But guess what? We do. We have Jesus Christ—our living taproot. The One who anchors us in love, truth, and unshakable purpose.

"... and provide for those who grieve in Zion— to bestow on them a crown of beauty instead of ashes, the oil of joy instead of mourning, and a garment of praise instead of a spirit of despair. They will be called oaks of righteousness, a planting of the Lord for the display of his splendor. ~ *Isaiah 61:3*

Did you get that? We are crowned, anointed, clothed, planted, and called *oaks of righteousness*! Let that settle in your spirit:

You are crowned, anointed, clothed, planted, and called.

You are not just here to survive—you are planted to display holy splendor.

Now consider this:

"... so that Christ may dwell in your hearts through faith. And I pray that you, being rooted and established in love, may have power, together with all the Lord's holy people, to grasp how wide and long and high and deep is the love of Christ, and to know this love that surpasses knowledge—that you may be filled to the measure of all the fullness of God."
~ *Ephesians 3:17-19*

Did you catch the sequence?
First, rooted. Then, filled.
Growth doesn't start with striving. It starts with anchoring —in His love, in His word, in His presence. You want to grow? You want to flourish? Then get low. Go deep. Root down. Let God do the underground work that no one sees. Because that's where your strength begins.

There's a temptation to only tend to what people can see—

our achievements, our appearance, our titles, our good deeds. But trees don't flourish from the top down. They grow from the roots up.

So let me ask you:

What are you rooted in right now?
What's feeding your strength—or stealing it?
Are your roots shallow or deep?
When life gets hard, what or who do you hold on to?

Maybe this is the season where you stop running, stop striving, and just root down. Anchor into the One who never moves. Trust that if you go deep, the fruit will come. It may take time. It may not look like what you expected. But friend, it will come.

Because you were planted with purpose. *It's time to Root Down to Rise Up.*

Garden Blessing

May your roots plunge deep into Christ's love, and may you stand firm like the oaks of righteousness, bearing fruit through every season.

Dirt Work Invitation: Strength Below the Surface

DRAW a tree on your Reflection page—any kind you like. Label the top portion *"Visible Me"* and the roots *"Invisible Me."*

On the Visible Me branches, write things others might see:
Your job, your roles, your smile, your strengths.
Then, at the roots, name what keeps you grounded:
Your faith, your prayers, your people, your quiet resilience,
your healing.
Ask yourself:

What (or Who) is my taproot?
Am I rooted deep enough to withstand a storm?

Next, write this declaration somewhere across the roots:

"I choose to root myself in Christ's love—so I
may grow strong, steady, and spirit-filled."

Close with this prayer:

Root me deep, Lord. Nourish me in the unseen places.

Reflection

_____
_____
_____
_____
_____
_____
_____
_____
_____
_____

11

MAKE TIME

"Bending by a storm can be a blessed new beginning."

What if falling is necessary in order to succeed? What if failing prepares us to grow stronger?

I always wondered about sayings like, "Sometimes when you lose, you win," or "No pain, no gain."

If falling, failing, and pain have the power to catapult us into a new, more desirable season, why do we fear the fall?

What if falling—or even failing—isn't a detour but the very path toward flourishing?

I've always wrestled with those well-meaning little sayings:

"Sometimes when you lose, you win."

"No pain, no gain."

"Failure is a stepping stone."

They sound good on mugs and motivational posters, but when you're in the middle of a fall—flat on your face, bent under pressure, or watching a dream dissolve—they don't always feel true.

And yet... what if they are?

What if the fall itself is the invitation to grow stronger roots?

I've shared before that I live with ADHD. Which means, quite literally, I cannot sit still. Stillness is an act of God in my world. I have two speeds: action and asleep—and absolutely nothing in between. For me, "relaxing" often looks like folding laundry, rearranging furniture, writing while stirring a pot of soup, or organizing the junk drawer while praying. I loathe sitting on the phone. Movies put me straight to sleep. And I always need something to do.

My mind is alive—always writing, imagining, dreaming. I see metaphors in the kitchen sink and storylines in my sons' cereal bowls.

Over time, I've learned creative ways to cope: I braid or twist my hair when I'm stuck on a call. I polish my nails during a movie so I don't completely drift. I invite friends to walk and talk instead of sit and chat.

But every now and then, God doesn't just nudge me to rest —He loving places me on *time-out*. A holy timeout. A mandatory pause. A red light I didn't see coming.

And strangely enough, I've always been grateful for those pauses. Every time God has slowed me down—whether through illness, transition, or sheer exhaustion—I've emerged more focused, more faithful, more rooted. He's shown me again and again that rest isn't a weakness. It's sacred work.

It took me years to learn how to just be.

To stop doing.

To stop fixing.

To stop rushing.

And where did I learn it best?

You guessed it: in the garden.

I MET Gail in a women's Bible study. We bonded quickly over our shared love of dirt, blooms, and spiritual metaphors. One afternoon, Gail invited me to see her garden—a space so thoughtfully designed it nearly brought me to tears. Every corner of her yard held intention, beauty, and quiet joy. She told me she began with an aerial view of her lot and carefully planned each section—how it would grow, what it would need, and how it would feel.

We wandered together through her garden paths, swapping stories. I told her about the vision God had given me for a garden-themed Bible study. I asked her what lessons she had learned while playing in the dirt.

She smiled. "Good dirt," she said first. "You need good dirt if you want anything to grow."

She then led me to her favorite flower: Cosmos.

I recognized them right away—simple petals, feathery leaves, standing tall and proud. She told me how hardy they were, how they returned each year in wild abundance.

She leaned in and I knew to listen carefully.

"One year," Gail said, pointing to a thick stalk, "a handful of my cosmos were knocked down. Bent all the way over. I thought they were done for. The stems weren't broken, but the flowers were pressed into the mulch, and I figured they'd rot or get eaten."

But she didn't pull them. She watched.

"And by the end of the week..." her eyes lit up, "they had sprouted new stalks. Right from the sides of the bent one. A single cosmos became twelve!"

I stood there in silence for a moment. Letting that settle.

Bent doesn't mean broken.
Knocked down doesn't mean done.
In fact, that's when the real growth can begin.

When life knocks us over, it often creates space for things we didn't plan—new shoots, new strength, new capacity. It's in the *bend* that we learn to let go, to rely on others, to cling to God, to release perfection. We learn to rest. We learn to receive.

SELF-CARE IS ALL the rage these days, but truthfully? It's nothing new. God invented it. Long before yoga mats and lavender bath bombs, the Creator of heaven and earth modeled the very first pause.

> "By the seventh day God had finished the work he had been doing; so on the seventh day he rested from all his work. Then God blessed the seventh day and made it holy, because on it he rested from all the work of creating that he had done." ∼ *Genesis* 2:2-3

Rest is not lazy.
Rest is not indulgent.
...Rest is holy.

SOMETIMES WE ARE ALLOWED to fall—not because we're being punished, but because we need to root deeper before we rise. Sometimes we are bent so that we can multiply. And sometimes, the season that looks like failure is actually a divine invitation to be still and let God work beneath the surface.

Garden Blessing

ᛣ

May every storm that bends you bring forth greater blooms. May you know that when you are bowed low, Heaven is sowing new seeds of abundance.

🌱 Dirt Work Invitation: Grown by Grace

TAKE a moment to think of a time when you felt knocked down—maybe you failed, stumbled, or were flat-out exhausted.

On one side of your Reflection page, write:

"Bent But Not Broken"

Underneath, name the moment and describe what it felt like. Then ask:

→ What did I learn from that experience?
→ How did God show up?
→ Did new growth eventually come?

NOW ON THE other side of the page, write:

"New Growth From the Fall"

List the ways that experience led to something unexpected: *Deeper wisdom? Compassion? A new opportunity? Greater faith?*

Then finish with this:

"Falling isn't the end. Sometimes it's the beginning of multiplied growth."

Optional Prompts

Draw a simple cosmos flower bent in the middle with new shoots rising from the bend—just like Gail's garden.

Use the Reflection page to think about the role of *rest* in your life. Are you well-rested? Describe what rest looks like for you. If you need rest, how can you carve out time for yourself?

REMEMBER THIS...

You are not broken.
You are becoming.

Reflection

_____

_____

_____

_____

_____

_____

_____

_____

_____

_____

PART 3

SUMMER

12

QUENCH YOUR THIRST

"There is a well that never runs dry, and His name is Jesus."

What if our thirst was finally quenched—not with what we want, but with what we need?

I always wondered what the long-term effects of living most of my life dehydrated would be.

I've spent most of my life thirsty.

Not just the literal kind of thirst, though I've certainly known that too. I mean the quiet, aching thirst of the soul. The kind that sneaks up on you in the middle of the night. The kind that lingers beneath the surface of your busyness and exhaustion. The thirst for comfort. Clarity. Connection. The thirst for peace when the pieces won't settle.

I've lived dehydrated.

Spiritually.

Emotionally.

Physically.

Far more often than I'd like to admit.

THE MORNING MY OLDEST SON, Trivé, was packed and ready to board a plane across the country for college, I woke up parched. My mouth was dry. My throat scratchy. My heart—heavy and bruised. I needed two things more than anything else in that moment: Jesus and water.

But I didn't reach for either.

Instead, I sank into the sheets and cried. Cried until I was sore. Until my body was empty. It wasn't that anything was wrong—he was ready, he was brave, he was leaving to chase his future. I was proud. Grateful. In awe of the young man we raised.

And I was utterly undone.

You see, I had given birth to him at twenty-six—a single mother with a fragile, premature baby and no roadmap for the life ahead. We did everything together, me and Trivé. We grew up in tandem. He could read my face like a book, catch my moods with a glance, and finish my sentences before I spoke them.

He wasn't just my son. He was my mirror. My witness. My anchor.

So when he left, something unrooted in me. I felt exposed. Like a limb had been quietly severed, and I didn't realize how much I depended on it until it was gone.

And in that sacred, sorrowful moment, I forgot to reach for the very things that could have carried me through: water... and the Word.

I dehydrated myself further with grief.

I lay still. I shut down. I withered.

I cannot go back to that moment, but I can choose differently next time. I can learn how to let God meet me in our thirst.

I REMEMBER the summer Indianapolis issued city-wide water restriction. Just one summer out of sixteen, but I'll never forget it. It was the only year we were banned from running our irrigation systems. The state was in near-drought. Farmers were on the brink of disaster. But me? I was staring out the window at my beautiful, blooming garden—and my crunchy, yellow grass.

It was awful.

I had done everything right that season. I had planned. I had planted. I had prepped the soil. I had finally gotten it all in place. And then... came the drought.

I was so desperate to save what I had built that I launched Project Midnight—a top-secret plan to run our sprinklers under the cover of darkness. I snuck around my house like a backyard burglar, whispering apologies to the Lord and imagining the consequences of being discovered by one of my neighbors—who happened to be a judge and a police detective. I was surrounded by the law, but determined to water my grass. I even practiced how I would explain why my grass was green: *it must be all of the trees and the shade...*

It was ridiculous. But I couldn't let it all go.

After one guilty night, I abandoned the plan and switched to hauling my largest watering can around the yard like a garden Sherpa, trying to hydrate "priority patches" of grass. It was laughable. And heartbreaking.

All I kept thinking was: Everything was right. I did everything right. All I needed was water.

. . .

HAVE you ever lived through a season like that? Where you did everything you were supposed to do. Where you prepared. You showed up. You obeyed. You poured out. And still—something dried up. Something fell apart. Something didn't bloom.

What did you do when it happened? Did you panic? Blame yourself? Power through? Shut down? I've been there. And what I've learned is this:

Even the best soil means nothing without living water.

THERE WILL BE seasons when we are prepared, equipped, aligned—and the rains still don't come. There will be seasons where we've done the inner work, but the external fruit is delayed. There will be moments when we beg for refreshment and feel only silence.

But don't miss this: sometimes, *thirst itself is the invitation.*
A holy ache.
A divine thirst.

A REMINDER that nothing can nourish like God can.

"God sets the lonely in families,
he leads out the prisoners with singing;
but the rebellious live in a sun-scorched land." ~ *Psalm 68:6*

That last line hits hard:
The rebellious live in a sun-scorched land.
It doesn't mean we're evil. Sometimes rebellion looks like self-reliance. Like forgetting to pray. Like trying to water our lives with things that were never meant to sustain us. Like

reaching for comfort before we reach for Christ.

But God, in His mercy, doesn't leave us there. He longs to refresh us. To restore us. To soak the dry places with living water.

GARDEN BLESSING

☘

May you be deeply rooted beside streams of Living Water, may your thirst be quenched with His love alone, and may drought never steal your song.

🖋 DIRT WORK INVITATION: QUENCHING THE RIGHT THIRST

ACROSS THE TOP of your Reflection page, write:

"Not Everything I Reach For Is What I Truly Need."

Now, divide the page in half.
On the left side, write:

"What I've Reached For When I'm Thirsty"

Be honest and unfiltered—snacks, social media, shopping, people-pleasing, busyness...
On the right side, write:

"What I Actually Needed"

Comfort, truth, connection, stillness, prayer, presence, Jesus...

Draw a droplet over the items on the right that deeply nourish your spirit.

Then pray:

> *"Lord, give me Living Water. Quench the thirst I don't always know how to name. Show me where I've turned to quick fixes, and gently lead me back to You."*

Reflection

_____

_____

_____

_____

_____

_____

_____

_____

_____

_____

13

BASK

"Without the Son, no soul can thrive."

What if the sun ceased to shine?

I always wondered what life would look like if the sun simply disappeared. I realize we wouldn't survive — but what would the day-by-day timeline be? Would flowers bow their heads first? Would the bees stop buzzing? What if there was no sunrise... no golden cast upon the morning sky... no warm patch of light streaming through your bedroom window? What if the sun simply didn't come and we walked in darkness?

IF I HAVEN'T SHARED or made it clear yet, my early years of gardening and landscaping were nothing short of a series of follies. I made every mistake possible — largely because I refused directions and still insisted on learning things for myself. I'd love to spin this in a more dignified way: Let's say I am a hands-on-learner. How's that?

Early in my yard and landscaping take-over, my husband commented on all of the patches of bare grass in our front yard. The month prior, I discharged our lawn care company for leaving grass clippings everywhere. Who knew that the spring clippings held seeds that made lawns healthier and fuller! Clearly, I didn't.

I also decided to make my own flower beds after I received a few outlandish estimates. It couldn't be that hard!? I noticed how the grass yellowed and died under a few bags of soil I left out. I didn't know how long it would take for the grass to die when denied sun, but I was certain that I could kill it without using chemicals. I made it my mission to grow grass in the patches David noted and to design two new flower beds in the back yard.

I thought the flower beds would be the most difficult of the two projects, but growing grass was harder than I expected. You see, grass needs sun and our patches were all shaded by our twenty-foot birch tree. I tried every shade variety available on the market, and each one would sprout and then curl up and die. I tried various mulching techniques, straw overlay, lawn starter soil, but the result was always the same. Dead grass.

On the other side of the house in full sun, the grass I covered with cardboard and bags of dirt took no time at all to die. At this point, I was tired of things dying — it was time to grow something, so I started digging my flower beds. In the end, the flower beds were stunning and I would eventually grow grass in the barren patches, but it took two years of trial and error. What ended up making the difference was cutting some of the branches on our birch tree back enough to allow the sun to peek through.

ONE DAY my youngest asked me what an oxymoron was. In trying to explain it, the first example that came to mind was an Alaskan-Garden. I'm sure there are gardens in Alaska, but my simplistic knowledge of the state only brought frozen and barren images of ice, snow, and months of darkness to mind. What can grow in darkness?

Years ago, a friend who is a pharmacist shared how disturbing she found the increase in depression prescriptions, particularly in the winter months. I have been very open about my struggles in the winter. Days upon days without sunshine and the bleak grey skies combined with the barren trees has a tremendous impact on my mood and outlook. Living in Indiana is only a bit better than Michigan, Wisconsin, and Illinois, but not by much. February is my blue month. It's the longest shortest month of every year.

The sun is so powerful and it's more than the Vitamin D. I believe it's deeper than that. The sun feeds our bones the way Jesus feeds our soul. I've certainly spent some unnecessary years in darkness — and in each instance, I was not growing in Christ. Sometimes, in order to grow, we don't need to do more — we need to let in more light. I have found that it is easy to get stuck in those awful shadows yet, oh so difficult to get unstuck. After all, it's hard to see in the dark.

GARDEN BLESSING

⚲

May the Light of Christ shine fully upon your heart. May the heavy shadows fall away, and may you bloom brightly beneath His gaze.

🌱 Dirt Work Invitation: Turn Toward the Light

BEGIN BY DRAWING A FLOWER — but instead of petals, let each petal be shaped like a sunbeam.

Inside each sunbeam, write a source of spiritual light in your life. Examples could be:

Scripture that nourishes you
Someone who uplifts your spirit
A place where you feel God's presence
A practice that fills you with peace

Now, draw a few "branches" hanging low over the flower — write on each one something that has blocked your light in this season. (These may be fears, habits, griefs, or even small distractions.)

Next, write:

"Lord, help me prune what blocks Your light. Make me bold enough to cut back what's no longer serving me. I want to grow. I want to thrive. I want to stand tall in Your Son-light."

Let this be your spiritual pruning season — not to punish, but to prepare you for new growth.

Reflection

_____
_____
_____
_____
_____
_____
_____
_____
_____
_____
_____

14

PRUNE WITH PURPOSE

"Even decrease is a kindness when it's made by the Gardener of your life."

What if less truly is more? I always wondered why we desire more yet purging is so satisfying. Pruning is one of my favorite lessons. Pruning was my first homeschool lesson with our oldest son. That's right, we started outside. I was knee-deep in gardening and had absolutely no idea what I was doing when it came to home- schooling. None! It was a last-minute decision after a summer of praying that our Lord would press a 'yes' upon my husband's heart.

I still remember when David appeared after a few hours of work in his home-office-man-cave and said that "We should home-school Trivé." Not, "Yes, you can do this,' but a, "We." No one will ever convince me that prayer does not change things... particularly when you are in alignment with our Lord's will.

IT WAS an early mid-August morning when I led Trivé (10 at the time) to our yard and handed him a pair of pruning shears. We sat on our sage green swing and looked at a few sad shrubs that lined the west side of the house. I asked him why he thought the lower half of the shrubs were barren compared to the lush upper portion. He offered amazing responses and was quick to note that the lower half wasn't getting any sun. He was right.

The bottom half of the shrubs were shaded and dense, so that's where our pruning lesson began. He spent a few hours cutting and reshaping the top of the shrubs while I hacked away branches of our oak tree until the sun was able to peek through and gaze upon the bushes.

In case you're wondering, many homeschool days that fall were spent outside. Trivé planted his own 2-foot cherry tree we picked up on clearance for $7 (which is now 20 feet tall). We learned so much together that year. We would spend that fall digging in, getting dirty, and planting lots of trees, plants, flowers, fruits and vegetables, and making splendid beautification plans.

I remember being thankful that my husband was not monitoring my garden expenses that year. With growth came waste.Or was it? Without the lessons, I wouldn't be writing this, now would I?

Many things were pruned during this season of exploration and growth. Many things died... and many things too, were born.

Before we talk about true pruning, let me tell you about the shrubs around our deck and my first season gardening. When we married, David had a lovely, large rust-colored deck and each side had two fairly mature shrubs that created a nice sense of privacy. Now David really liked those shrubs.

As I wandered through my new space, I noted that several of the shrubs around the deck were discolored and spotted,They must be diseased, I thought. I was mortified... diseases spread! There was only one thing to do: cut them down. The shrubs had to go.

The next morning, I suited up in all the protective gear I could find and dug up every single shrub and threw each one in the dumpster. I'm shaking my head now as I recall my husband's dismay when he returned home from a work-trip and saw that they were gone! I can't say I noticed then... or perhaps I didn't care. The thought of disease was the end of that discussion.

TEN YEARS LATER, I wondered if they were truly diseased... or just in need of pruning. Maybe they just needed more sun, or a little extra care. I can say with full honesty that while I created beautiful gardens in nearly every corner of our yard, the space around that deck? Remained barren until the day we moved.

That's what I want you to remember: Pruning should never be done in haste.

True pruning is thoughtful. Observant. Purposeful.

Some things must be cut off — immediately and completely.

Others? They need only to be trimmed back, given breathing room, shaped with love.

We must learn to tell the difference.

"I am the true vine, and my Father is the gardener. He

cuts off every branch in me that bears no fruit, while
every branch that does bear fruit he prunes so that it
will be even more fruitful. You are already clean
because of the word I have spoken to you. Remain in
me, as I also remain in you. No branch can bear fruit by
itself; it must remain in the vine. Neither can you bear
fruit unless you remain in me." ~ *John 15:1-4*

Jesus didn't say He cuts off bad branches and leaves the
good alone.

He prunes fruitful branches — so they'll bear even more
fruit.

Sometimes the thing that needs pruning is not bad at all —
it may be good; *but it's not God's best for you in this season.*

Maybe it's a relationship that needs new boundaries.

A commitment that began purpose, but is now stunting
your growth.

A title, identity, or dream that no longer reflects who you're
becoming.

Pruning can look like a job shift, a cleared calendar, or a
simpler life.

And pruning always makes room for more fruit — more
of Him.

GARDEN BLESSING

May you have the courage to prune what hinders your light, and the wisdom to trust the hands of the Master Gardener. May your branches grow heavy with holy fruit.

🌱 DIRT WORK INVITATION: PRUNE WITH PURPOSE

TAKE a blank sheet of paper and draw a bush or tree with 5–7 branches.

🌷 Label each branch with something in your life that is taking your time, energy, or attention right now. Include the "good" things too.

🌷 Now, using a colored pen or pencil, circle the branches that are bearing fruit — things in your life that are bringing growth, peace, connection, or clarity.

🌷 Put a small mark next to the ones that may need pruning — not out of guilt, but out of growth.

Then reflect and write:

→ What areas of my life might need gentle pruning?

→ What's crowding my spirit or blocking the light?

→ What would fruitfulness look like in this next season?

Finally, pray this aloud:

Lord, I surrender what no longer serves my growth in You. Teach me the art of pruning — with wisdom, grace, and courage. I trust that even in letting go, You are making room for more fruit.

Reflection

_____

_____

_____

_____

_____

_____

_____

_____

_____

_____

_____

15

GIRD UP

"Tender gardens need strong gates and faithful armor."

What if fences keep in just as much as they keep out? I always wondered about gated communities and what or who they were keeping out? Shortly after moving into our current home, we built a gate on the east side of the house. Our intent was to have a place where our three dogs could run and play without the worry of one of them darting off after a rabbit or squirrel.

Initially we had an estimate done for the cost of gating our entire yard (which would have required a second mortgage).When flags were placed to show us where the gate would be, I sat on our deck and looked out in disapproval. I could see the smooth lines of the cast iron fence and loved the way it accented our coal black roof, but I couldn't get past the closed-in-feeling. It was almost suffocating. Our sprawling lush yard would be interrupted with this divider. A once natural land-scape would be cut and remind everyone that 'this over here and everything inside the iron bars was ours.' Only... everything inside the bars was ours, we didn't need a gate to make it so.

MY YOUNGEST SON is now a teenager, but as a toddler and child he was an eloper (common in the ASD community). After multiple near fatal incidents, I reconsidered tethering him to me when we were out (using a leash). Before being a parent, I shook my head hen I saw children walking about the Windy City on a leash. How dehumanizing, I thought to myself. It would take watching my child dash off down our cul-de-sac and seeing the fast-approaching delivery truck steered by what looked like another child to make me understand that some children need some things for their own protection.

I love those kinds of lessons — when I can look back and see how strongly I felt about something only later to realize my assessments were based on little to no experience or knowledge on the matter. There is power in genuinely adopting a 'seek to understand' approach to that which we do not agree. Are fences or gated communities 'wrong'? Absolutely not. For some, they offer safety and protection.

AFTER FIRING ALL the lawn help, it would take a few years before I figured out that I needed to treat my lawn and flower beds. Weed prevention pellets, lawn fertilizers, slug prevention granules, and insect repellants were all new to me, but each was necessary and offered a different type of protection that we needed.

I learned how much better our grass did when I over-seeded and applied fall weed preventions; that with three dogs, slug prevention was necessary every spring; and, that if we wanted to enjoy evenings laughing around the fire pit without getting eaten by mosquitos and friends, it would be important to apply repellant monthly. I learned to protect.

Prevention is a form of protection. If you've experienced the problems caused by identity theft, you know that prevention is key. Once it's done, it can take years to fully correct and repair. In the same manner, weed prevention in the fall requires you to think ahead about the upcoming spring and not to wait for those pesky broad leafs to appear. Once weeds root, it's a whole different ball game.

DID you know that the presence of weeds and thorns came as a consequence of Adam and Eve eating from the forbidden tree:

"Cursed is the ground because of you through painful toil you will eat food from it all the days of your life. It will produce thorns and thistles for you, and you will eat the plants of the field. By the sweat of your brow you will eat your food until you return to the ground, since from it you were taken; for dust you are and to dust you will return." ~ *Genesis 3:17-19*

Jesus had a few things to say about weeds as well:

"The one who sows the good seed is the Son of Man, the field is the world, and the good seed are the children of the kingdom; the weeds are the children of the evil one, and the enemy who sowed them is the devil; the harvest is the end of the age, and the reapers are angels." ~ *Matthew 13:37-39*

Weeds are fascinating. In my first few years of gardening, I mistook several weeds for flowers because they were flowering! It wasn't until one in particular grew taller than our garage that I decided to find out what this flowering giant was.

Isn't it interesting that some weeds look just like some wild-flowers. For example, I have flowers that look exactly like dandelions. I thought about why one was welcome, cut, vased, and placed on a credenza and the other was yanked out, dug up, or sprayed with chemicals we hoped would kill it. The answer was found beneath the soil where I gained an under-standing of how deep weed roots grow, and how easily and quickly they spread.

The Armor of God

"Finally, be strong in the Lord and in his mighty power.
Put on the full armor of God, so that you can take your
stand against the devil's schemes. For our struggle is not
against flesh and blood, but against the rulers, against
the authorities, against the powers of this dark world
and against the spiritual forces of evil in the heavenly
realms. Therefore put on the full armor of God, so that
when the day of evil comes, you may be able to stand
your ground, and after you have done everything, to
stand. Stand firm then, with the belt of truth buckled
around your waist, with the breastplate of
righteousness in place, and with your feet fitted with
the readiness that comes from the gospel of peace. In
addition to all this, take up the shield of faith, with
which you can extinguish all the flaming arrows of the
evil one. Take the helmet of salvation and the sword of
the Spirit, which is the word of God."
~ Ephesians 6:10-17

"Put on the full armor of God...
so that when the day of evil comes,
you may be able to stand your ground..."
~ Ephesians 6:13

A FEW YEARS AGO, I told my husband I felt under attack.
My thoughts were sharp with shame. My confidence was
nowhere to be found. I was spiraling in self-loathing and didn't
know how to stop the storm.

The next morning, as I got dressed, I glanced up at a

picture he had hung in our closet — an ancient knight, fully suited in armor, labeled with every piece described in Ephesians.

It wasn't just decorative. It was directive.

A reminder that I wasn't meant to fight alone or unarmed.

The enemy doesn't need to climb over your fence if you've already let weeds grow from within. The armor of God protects from the inside out.

Garden Blessing

May the boundaries you build be blessed, may they shelter joy and shield peace, and may you suit up daily in the full armor of God.

🌱 Dirt Work Invitation: Suit Up & Weed Out

FIND a quiet moment and grab a sheet of paper. Draw a simple figure of yourself in the middle of the page. Around the figure, label the parts of the Armor of God (Ephesians 6:10–17):

Belt of Truth

Breastplate of Righteousness

Shoes of Peace

Shield of Faith

Helmet of Salvation

Sword of the Spirit

NOW REFLECT:

Which pieces am I wearing daily? Which have I left behind?

Where do I need greater protection — in my heart, thoughts, faith, or actions?

Where have weeds rooted in my life? What's pretending to be a flower but choking out my joy?

THEN WRITE A PERSONAL PRAYER:

Lord, help me recognize the difference between a boundary and a barrier. Guard my thoughts, protect my peace, and guide me in truth. Show me what needs pulling, pruning, or replacing.And suit me up in Your armor — every single day.

Reflection

_____
_____
_____
_____
_____
_____
_____
_____
_____
_____

16

TIME FOR A BIGGER POT

"New roots need new room to stretch toward heaven."

I always wondered how I'd know when a plant of mine had outgrown its pot. Was there a way to tell before distress set in? Turns out, there are signs: if it stops growing or if it shows signs of distress, like yellow or brown leaves.

That's it. Simple.

But when it comes to our own lives, we often miss the cues. We keep pushing, producing, showing up — not realizing we're root-bound and stunted by our current container.

Somewhere on my personal Top 10 Films list is Big Fish (2003), a visually rich and tender story adapted from Daniel Wallace's novel *Big Fish: A Novel of Mythic Proportions*. The film is part fable, part love story, and a meditation on story-telling, legacy, and the truth we find in myth.

One moment has always stayed with me: the idea that a fish will only grow as big as its pond allows. Place a fish in a small bowl, and it will stay small. But put it in a bigger body of water, and it will grow into what it was meant to become.

Is this scientific? Symbolic?

Maybe both.

Either way, I believe the same is true for you and me. We cannot reach our fullness in a space too small for our calling. Our roots need depth. Our gifts need stretching. Our dreams need margin. Growth requires room.

DID you know carrots come in a rainbow of colors?

I didn't. But once I did, I was all in. I spotted a catalog ad for purple and yellow carrots and immediately ordered the seeds. I had big plans for this harvest: glazed purple carrots on the table, golden shredded carrots over fresh salad, and extra bags to hand out to the neighbors — who would, no doubt, be in awe of my rainbow veggie bounty.

I decided to try box gardening, a popular trend at the time. I assembled my wooden square — mostly by feel (still not reading directions), lined the bottom with organic weed liner, filled it with rich, store-bought soil, and dropped in the seeds. My dreams were as rich as the dirt.

Weeks passed, and the green shoots finally arrived — lush, leafy, tall. I was thrilled. I couldn't wait any longer. Baby carrots were my favorite anyway. I reached down, wrapped my fingers around the leafy top, and pulled.

What emerged was... unforgettable.

What I held in my hand could only be described as a carrot meatball — a short, fat, rolled-up nugget of orange confusion. My mouth literally dropped open. It looked like something from a Dr. Seuss nightmare garden.

What happened? I had done everything right:

The right dirt.
The right light.
The right water.
The right seeds.
The right planter.

But my carrots had no space to grow.

The very thing I used to protect the box — that organic weed liner — blocked the carrots' roots from pushing down into the earth. The liner created a barrier between the good dirt above and the nutrient-rich clay below.

My carrots had a place, but not space.

HAVE you ever found yourself in the right place — the perfect job, relationship, community, or opportunity — and yet felt stuck?

Unmotivated?

Invisible?

Tired all the time for no reason at all?

That's how you know.

The environment might be beautiful. It may have looked like the right fit. You may have even chosen it with wisdom and prayer. But that doesn't mean it was meant for your long-term growth. Sometimes, we're placed somewhere to begin... *not to stay.*

A pot has a purpose, but it also has a limit.

Growth can't continue where there is no space for roots to deepen, ideas to stretch, or spirits to breathe.

Jesus never promised that the soil would always be soft. But He did talk a lot about where seeds fall:

"Still other seed fell on good soil. It came up and yielded a crop,
a hundred times more than was sown." ~ *Luke 8:8*

If we desire to yield a life rich in fruit — love, joy, peace,
patience, and purpose — we must be planted where our roots
can spread.

You are not selfish for needing space.

You are not broken for outgrowing what once fit.

You are not faithless for uprooting what stunts your growth.

Your root health determines your fruit health.

GARDEN BLESSING

☥

*May the walls around your heart expand to make
room for every new thing God wants to plant. May
you stretch wide in faith, and grow wildly free.*

🌱 DIRT WORK INVITATION: MAKE ROOM TO GROW

TAKE out your journal or use the Reflection page. At the top,
write:

"A Place vs. Space"

Draw a simple two-column chart. On the left, list all the
places in your life right now — literal and symbolic:

Home

Work

Church

Friend circles
Family roles
Hobbies

THEN ON THE RIGHT, reflect honestly:

*Does this place give me space to grow? Am I still
thriving here... or just surviving? What feels root-bound?
What might need repotting?*

Finally, write a prayer of bold release and gentle
realignment:

Lord, give me the eyes to see where I've outgrown the
pots I once prayed for. Help me know when it's time to
uproot and when it's time to push deeper. Expand the
borders of my spirit. Grant me space for the growth
You intend. Make room in me... and all around me.
Amen.

Reflection

_____
_____
_____
_____
_____
_____
_____
_____
_____
_____
_____

17

GO

"Trust the Hands that move you and knows the good soil ahead."

What if growth and healing are waiting — just one brave move away?

I always wondered why we stay in toxic environments far longer than we should. Why don't we pack up and move when something no longer serves us — or worse, when it harms us? But now I know: relocation is a luxury. It requires more than a suitcase and a bold spirit. It requires resources, readiness, courage, and clarity — things we often lack when we're weary and wounded.

Still, the truth remains: sometimes the soil you're planted in can no longer support your healing.

For months, I avoided writing this lesson.

Transplanting isn't just a gardening principle. It's a spiritual act, and one of the hardest God ever calls us to do. It means leaving something familiar. Even when the environment is stifling or harmful, we cling to it because it's what we know.

MANY YEARS AGO, I was transitioning from one position to another at a small Christian school. The shift was prompted by a year of difficulty — my leadership role had stirred tension with colleagues, and though I loved the students deeply, I was becoming someone I didn't recognize. I felt misunderstood, boxed in, and tired.

Stepping down into a new, supportive role was my idea. I thought it would allow healing to begin. But beneath it all, I knew I was being called to leave altogether. I knew my season there was over. But I lingered. I argued with God. I insisted my students still needed me. I told myself reconciliation had to come first. I said I wasn't finished yet.

The Holy Spirit was clear. "Go."

But I wasn't ready to obey.

And so, my peace withered. Everything became heavier. The year that followed was one of the most painful of my professional life. I saw things I can't unsee. Relationships broke. Conflicts escalated. My spirit wilted under the weight of disobedience. I knew better. *I wasn't supposed to be there.*

WHY DO I stall when God says "Go"? Why do I resist divine assignments, even when I know they are good?

Because they are also hard.

Because I don't feel equipped.

Because I want to know the plan before I take the first step.

...But that's not how faith works.

"By faith Abraham, when called to go to a place he would later receive as his inheritance, obeyed and went, even though he did not know where he was going." ~ *Hebrews 11:8*

Abraham didn't ask God for a five-point itinerary. He didn't negotiate. He just went. That's faith. And I've longed to have that kind of trust. But time and time again, I've clung to my comfort, ignoring the dry, depleted soil beneath me.

ONE SPRING AFTERNOON, I learned the lesson of transplanting through a little Japanese Maple in my backyard.

She was struggling. The sun was too harsh in her current spot, and her leaves were withering. I knew she needed to be moved to the shaded side of the yard. But when I started digging her up, she resisted. Her roots had wrapped themselves tightly into the ground, and she fought every tug. I watered the base. I coaxed her gently. But she wouldn't budge.

I sat there, muddy and exhausted, and did something new — I spoke to my tree.

"I know you probably don't understand why I'm doing this," I whispered. "I know you like it here. I know it's familiar. But you're not going to make it if you stay. You're burning up. You're too exposed — and I want you to live."

With one final push of my shovel, she released. The root ball rose. It was a beautifully divine gardening experience. I couldn't help but think of how many times the Lord whispered that same thing to me.

I want you to live.

"He lifted me out of the slimy pit,
out of the mud and mire;
he set my feet on a rock

and gave me a firm place to stand." ~ *Psalm* 40:2

Sometimes, in order to heal, you have to leave. Not because you're weak or selfish or giving up, but because the soil you're in can no longer sustain your growth.

God is not afraid of our questions. He welcomes them. But ultimately when He says "Go," He is saying, "Trust me."

He is saying *I want you to live.*

Garden Blessing

May you trust the hands of the Master Gardener when He says, "It's time to move. May you bloom even more brightly in your new soil.

⚘ DIRT WORK INVITATION: ARE YOU ROOT-BOUND?

USE your reflection page to explore this deeply personal question:

Where am I being called to uproot and move?

Draw a small potted plant. Label the container with the names of any space or situation that feels constricted right now:

A job

A ministry

A friend group

A church

A mindset

A habit

A fear

Now draw roots reaching out from the base — but have them press up against the pot's edges, showing no room to stretch.

Ask yourself:

Are these roots tangled and bound?
What would it feel like to be lifted and placed some-
where with room to expand?
What's one brave next step you could take?

Questions we are unsure how to answer — submit to our Lord. His will for you is perfect, but we often struggle with what steps to take. I know I do. I want a telegram with a numbered list of instructions. My answer is 'yes', but I can get stuck on the minute details. I've learned to submit my questions and pray for wisdom and discernment as I GO and step toward His will for me.

Pray this aloud:

Lord, I want to heal. I want to grow.
But I confess I've grown too comfortable in places that
no longer feed me.
Show me where You are calling me to go.
Strengthen my faith to obey without a map.
Let my roots stretch wide in the soil You've prepared.
Let me live. Amen.

> "I waited patiently for the Lord;
> he turned to me and heard my cry.
> He lifted me out of the slimy pit,
> out of the mud and mire;
> he set my feet on a rock
> and gave me a firm place to stand.

He put a new song in my mouth,
a hymn of praise to our God.
Many will see and fear the Lord
and put their trust in him."

~ Psalm 40:1-3

Reflection

_____

_____

_____

_____

_____

_____

_____

_____

_____

_____

18

PLAY IN THE DIRT

"Healing is not surface work; it is holy excavation."

What if our outside accurately represented our insides?

I always wondered what would be visible if my outer appearance matched the contents of my heart.

Would there be patches of beauty?

Would there be scathing brokenness?

Probably both.

There were times in my life I wished for someone—anyone—to see through the curated version of me. I wondered if anyone could sense the spiritual bruises, the soul-fractures that polite conversation could never touch. I walked through seasons so fragmented, yet still managed to slap on lipstick and say, "I'm good."

We all have hidden caverns within—

Wounds we haven't tended.

Questions we haven't answered.

Hurts we buried so deep we forgot they still bleed.

Sometimes, instead of seeking true healing, we learn to perform. We learn to present. We learn to build better facades. We wear the bright colors. We take care of everyone else. We light the candle, fluff the throw pillows, and paint the deck.

But covering decay doesn't stop it.

I learned this — painfully — in our old backyard.

Our wooden deck was beginning to soften and sag. Each spring, wood-boring bees swarmed and nested in the fading planks. When I asked a home improvement specialist what to do, he told me that a few coats of latex paint would seal things up and keep the bees away. It sounded simple enough. And it worked... for a season.

But deep down, I knew better.

Under the thick, heavy coats of paint, the rot was still there... and spreading. The wood was already compromised. My effort to cover the damage didn't make it disappear — it made it worse. In time, the bees returned. But this time, so did the infestation. It was no longer just a nuisance — it was structural. The entire deck had been hollowed out by a sophisticated wood-burrowing bee empire. The inner deck was destroyed.

How many times had I done the same with my life?

Covered pain with productivity.

Covered heartbreak with hospitality.

Covered fear with faith-flavored phrases I didn't fully believe at the time.

I tried to "paint" myself whole.

But friends, Band-Aids and décor don't heal gaping wounds. There's no shortcut to deep restoration. True healing is slow. Sometimes messy. Often sacred.

We can't paint over brokenness. We can't dress up decay.

We need the Carpenter.

We need the Healer.

We need Jesus.

The rot must be exposed so the rebuilding can begin. And while exposure can feel vulnerable, shameful, or even terrifying — it is also the most courageous act of surrender.

I believe this with my whole heart: God is not interested in your performance. He desires your presence. He doesn't need your "togetherness," He wants your truth. He already sees what's under the paint—and still, He loves you. Still, He chooses you. Still, He invites you closer.

> "Create in me a pure heart, O God,
> and renew a steadfast spirit within me." ~ Psalm 51:10

Garden Blessing

May you allow the Master Carpenter to rebuild every cracked and hollow place. May the beauty He forms within shine so brightly, there's no need

Dirt Work Invitation: TIME TO DIG

IT'S time to get honest—with God, with yourself. Forget about house damage and that bee-ridden deck. Take it home:

→ Where is the rot in your life that you slapped a bandaid on and kept going?

→ Is there a place where you need healing, but have only allowed surface-level solutions?

Peeling back this bandaid is one of the more challenging

and revealing tasks, but I am urging you to do it anyway — fall is coming.

CLOSE YOUR EYES and ask the Spirit to walk with you into that "deck" space. What do you sense God is inviting you to uncover or surrender?

LET this be the season you stop painting over the rot. Let this be the season you allow God to rebuild what was never meant to be carried alone.

Psalm 139

O LORD, you have searched me and you know me.
You know when I sit and when I rise; you perceive my thoughts from afar.
You discern my going out and my lying down; you are familiar with all my ways.
Before a word is on my tongue you know it completely, O LORD.
You hem me in—behind and before; you have laid your hand upon me.
Such knowledge is too wonderful for me, too lofty for me to attain.
Where can I go from your Spirit? Where can I flee from your presence?
If I go up to the heavens, you are there; if I make my bed in the depths, you are there.
If I rise on the wings of the dawn, if I settle on the far side of the sea,
even there your hand will guide me, your right hand will hold me fast.
If I say, "Surely the darkness will hide me and the light become night around me,"
even the darkness will not be dark to you; the night will shine like the day, for darkness is as light to you.
For you created my inmost being; you knit me together in my mother's womb.
I praise you because I am fearfully and wonderfully made; your works are wonderful, I know that full well.
My frame was not hidden from you when I was made in the secret place. When I was woven together in the depths of the earth,
your eyes saw my unformed body. All the days ordained for me were written in your book before one of them came to be.
How precious to me are your thoughts, O God! How vast is the sum of them!
Were I to count them, they would outnumber the grains of sand. When I awake, I am still with you.
If only you would slay the wicked, O God! Away from me, you bloodthirsty men!
They speak of you with evil intent; your adversaries misuse your name.
Do I not hate those who hate you, O LORD, and abhor those who rise up against you?
I have nothing but hatred for them; I count them my enemies.
Search me, O God, and know my heart; test me and know my anxious thoughts.
See if there is any offensive way in me, and lead me in the way everlasting.

Reflection

_____

_____

_____

_____

_____

_____

_____

_____

_____

_____

PART 4

FALL

19

PLAN FOR THE FALL

"A wise gardener stores joy for winter's lean days."

What if I prepared for my annual bout of seasonal depression?

I always wondered how to face the dark, dreary months of fall and winter without falling into despair.

For years, I dreaded the slow approach of autumn. Most people saw cozy sweaters, pumpkin-scented candles, and foliage in a thousand hues. I saw the shadows lengthening. I felt the sunlight slipping away. I braced for what I knew was coming:

Shorter days.

Endless gray skies.

That hollow stillness that swells in the pit of February.

Every September, when the first gold edges appeared on the leaves of our pear tree, a wave of dread would wash over me. I could feel it in my bones. The light was leaving.

I tried everything to outpace it.

Some years, I leaned on medication.

Some years, I doubled down on productivity.

Some years, I isolated and suffered in silence, trying to "push through" — trying to fake joy when all I actually felt was dread.

But the year I finally named it — Seasonal Depression — something shifted. Naming it gave it less power. Denial was no longer an option. Neither was doing nothing.

So, I made a plan.

I gave myself permission to prepare — the same way I would prepare my garden each fall. I realized my sadness wasn't weakness. It was a signpost. A cue. A knowing that deserved to be honored, not ignored.

Just like bulbs need to be planted in fall to bloom in spring...

Just like mulch must be laid to protect the roots during winter's chill...

I too needed a plan that would sustain me until the sun returned.

Once I named it, sharing my seasonal blues became easy. What I didn't expect was how many others struggled as well. I decided to write a short eBook during one of those low seasons: "7 Tips to Conquer Seasonal Depression". It wasn't meant to be prescriptive. It was meant to be personal — a map back to myself. I wanted to share what helped me most.

→ Talk About It

Don't hide. Share your struggle with trusted friends or a therapist. Don't let shame grow in the dark.

→ Meaningful Projects

Distraction doesn't have to be mindless. Pour yourself into work or creativity that gives you joy or purpose.

→ Acts of Kindness

Helping others gently pulls us from the pit. Serve someone. You'll both be lifted.

→ Plan a Getaway

Have something warm and beautiful to look forward to —even if it's small.

→ Reconnect with Friends

Isolation feeds depression. Reach out. Say yes to coffee. Answer the phone.

→ Journal Honestly

Let your feelings out, unfiltered and free. God's not afraid of your sadness.

→ Learn Something New

Let yourself grow—even in winter. Especially in winter.

DOING nothing wasn't loving myself. I began treating my fall like a farmer would:

Prepping the soil.
Mulching the roots.
Covering the beds.
Planting bulbs that would sleep beneath the surface,
waiting to rise.
Fall fertilization is for future flourishing.

What I do now determines how I will bloom later.

"There is a time for everything, and a season for every activity under the heavens." ~ *Ecclesiastes* 3:1

Garden Blessing
☥

May you make peace with your seasons, and prepare your heart for both the quiet and the bloom. May your fall be fertilized with hope.

🌱 Dirt Work Invitation: Ready, Prep, Go!

LET this season be one of gentleness and preparation.

1. What are your early warning signs that "the fall" is approaching — emotionally, spiritually, physically?

2. What could your fall-prep plan include this year? Write 2–3 ideas that feel tender and true.

3. How does your fall season mirror your spiritual life? Is there something God is asking you to lay down and cover, to nourish quietly in the dark?

ASK the Gardener of your soul to help you trust the dormant seasons.

You may not be blooming, but oh, you are growing.

Reflection

_____

_____

_____

_____

_____

_____

_____

_____

_____

20

REMEMBER

"Your alabaster box holds all the treasure He desires – your heart."

What if the very thing we've been searching for has been inside us all along?

I always wondered if the desires of our hearts were actually... in our hearts. Maybe we don't have to roam the world looking for peace, purpose, or provision. Maybe we just need to remember who we are—and Whose we are.

As believers, we are called to a sacred rhythm of remembrance. Communion is not simply tradition; it is nourishment for our souls.

"After taking the cup, he gave thanks and said, 'Take
this and divide it among you. For I tell you I will not
drink again from the fruit of the vine until the kingdom
of God comes.' And he took bread, gave thanks and
broke it, and gave it to them, saying, 'This is my body
given for you; do this in remembrance of me.' In the
same way, after the supper he took the cup, saying,
'This cup is the new covenant in my blood, which is
poured out for you.'" ~ Luke 22:17–20

Jesus asked us to remember. Not just once. Continually.
Ritually. Fully. We are to: Remember. Return. And Remain.

I believe He knew the power of memory. He knew that to
remember is to not forget — and that forgetting is what keeps us
lost.

It sounds so simple, *but it isn't*.

———

WHEN MY BROTHER, James-Kious, passed in 2020, the
grief that followed was unlike anything I'd known. There were
days I couldn't find the energy to stand. People flooded me with
texts, cards, and posts — many of them including the phrase:
"Gone, but not forgotten."

Every time I read those words, I flinched. "Gone" was too
small a word. Too sterile. Too quiet to contain the sound of my
heartbreak. But it was the second part that lingered: *not
forgotten*.

For a while, I waited for healing to feel like forgetting. I
thought time would make the memories fade or that remem-
bering would become less painful. But one day, I saw his smile
in my mind's eye. I heard him laugh. And I didn't cry. I felt
warmth. Joy. Grief and grace danced together.

That's when I realized healing doesn't mean forgetting. *Healing is the ability to remember without breaking.*

So I decided I would remember on purpose. I would speak his name. Tell his stories. Play our favorite songs while driving. I would carry his memory forward like a torch. Even if it hurt.

Even if it healed.

WE ARE CREATURES OF RHYTHM. We remember best what we return to often. Just like muscle memory trains the body, spiritual memory trains the soul. Whether it's a passcode or a prayer, repetition roots us.

Communion. Repetition. Return.

Do this in remembrance of Me...

Not just once. But again. And again. And again.

I SEE this in my garden photography too. Every season, I walk through my flowerbeds with camera in hand. I capture what worked, what thrived, what inspired me. In winter, I return to those images — not just to admire them but to remember the design, the intention, the beauty that once bloomed ...*and can bloom again.*

My garden photo journal is affectionately called *My Alabaster Box.* And in it, I place not only pictures of flowers, but visions, memories, —offerings.

It is both a record and a promise.

A memory of *what was* and a preparation for *what will be.*

MY ALL-TIME favorite Christmas song is "The Little Drummer Boy." And no matter how many times I hear it, I cry.

We learn that the boy has nothing "fit to give our King." No gold, no gift — just his drum. So he plays his best for Jesus. And the line that breaks me every time?

"Then He smiled at me."

That's it.

That's what we're after. The smile of our Savior. The approval of the One who sees what we offer — no matter how simple — and says, "That's beautiful."

I see myself in that boy. Poor in possessions. Unworthy in offerings. But what I do have... I give.

MY GARDEN IS MY DRUM.

My writing is my song.

THESE ARE the contents of my alabaster box.

They may not be "fit" for a King — and others may see my gifts as insufficient, but they are mine. And I pour them out at His feet with love.

"When she poured this perfume on my body, she did it to prepare me for burial.
Truly I tell you, wherever this gospel is preached throughout the world,
what she has done will also be told, in memory of her." ∼
Matthew 26:12–13

GARDEN BLESSING

⚲

May your hands never be too full to offer what's in your alabaster box. May you pour freely, and may Heaven catch every drop.

🌱 DIRT WORK INVITATION: WHAT'S IN YOUR ALABASTER BOX?

TODAY, we remember.
Remember what you've given.
Remember what you've grown.
Remember what you've lost — and what you still carry.

USE your Reflection page to fill your own Alabaster Box.
Draw a small jar or box and write inside it:

→ What do you have to offer?
→ What gifts or talents feel "unworthy," but are wholly and sincerely yours?
→ What memories are you holding close — what do you choose to remember?

Next, ask yourself:

→ What does remembrance look like in my life?
→ How can I make space to remember God's faithfulness, to reflect, to honor, to give thanks?

LASTLY, offer this prayer aloud or in writing:

Jesus, I remember.
I remember You — Your sacrifice, Your love, Your smile.
I offer what I have, simple and sincere.
Help me pour out my gifts without shame or hesitation.
Let my offerings bring You joy.
And may I always, always choose to remember.

Reflection

_____

_____

_____

_____

_____

_____

_____

_____

_____

_____

_____

21

BE STILL

"Bloom bravely where your Gardener has planted you."

I always wondered why we spend so much time thinking about the future—what's next, what's missing, what needs fixing. We do this so much that we often forget where we are. We miss this moment. *The only moment that is guaranteed.*

That thought makes my heart race because I know it's true: *This moment will never return.*

Once it's gone, it's gone.

Loss is the teacher that reveals this truth with piercing clarity. It's not until something—or someone—is gone that we remember the way they laughed, the way the light hit the table just right at dinner, the scent of spring creeping through the window. The way we took it all for granted.

The sacred ordinary.

. . .

THIS BOOK IS DIVIDED into seasons for a reason. Seasons anchor me. They remind me that this moment matters—not someday, not when things calm down, not after we fix it all. *Today.*

The choices I make today cultivate and fertilize the tomorrow I long for. But the truth is, today is the miracle.

This season is the gift we often can't see. Even if it's messy, slow, or bittersweet.

Fall is the time of harvest. Of beauty and letting go. As the leaves fall, and the garden fades, it's easy to feel like we're losing something. But that's not the whole story.

Fall isn't an ending.

Fall is a sacred shift.

AS FALL COMES to a close and winter approaches, enter the new season with joy. Enter it with a sacred resolve to rest.

Yes, rest.

With all the love in my heart, I am telling you—no, I am blessing you—to *rest.*

Winter is the season for stillness, for recovery, for sacred silence. It's a time to remember who you are and who God has always been. If you've never done Priscilla Shirer's *Breathe* study, winter is the perfect time. Because life will do what it does.

Leaves will fall.
Annuals will die.
Perennials will retreat underground.
But not you.
You are still growing.
You are getting stronger.
Your roots are gripping deeper.
You have lived and learned.
You've tilled and toiled.
You've wept, laughed, prayed, and pressed forward.
You are a mighty oak,
Rooted in truth,
Anchored in love,
Planted in the promises of God.

"Blessed is the one who does not walk in step with the wicked
or stand in the way that sinners take
or sit in the company of mockers,
but whose delight is in the law of the Lord,
and who meditates on his law day and night.
That person is like a tree planted by streams of water,
which yields its fruit in season
and whose leaf does not wither—
whatever they do prospers." ~ *Psalm 1:1–3*

You are that tree. Even now. Even in winter. Even in your waiting.
Planted.
Nourished.
Unshakable.
You are the blessed one. Your roots are not withering—they're holding fast.

"He will cover you with his feathers,
and under his wings you will find refuge;
his faithfulness will be your shield and rampar~ *Psalm 91:4*

So make time.
Not for hustle. Not for striving.
Make time to be still.
Find a quiet place that calms your spirit.
Sit there.
Let the sun pour in or the snow quietly fall.
Let the silence remind you of how safe you are.
Set your list aside. Unclench your jaw.
Unwrinkle your forehead. Open your hands.
God is here.
Be still long enough to hear the whisper that changes
everything.

GARDEN BLESSING
☥

May you stand strong through every season, planted firmly by the waters of His Word. May your roots grow deeper, your branches wider, and your heart forever anchored in His love.

🌱 Dirt Work Invitation 21: Rest, Remember, Root

THIS IS your invitation to settle into this sacred season and trust that you are exactly where you should be.

On your reflection page, respond to the following prompts:

WHAT HAS *this devotional journey revealed to me?*
What am I harvesting from this season of my life?
What parts of me need rest, not more effort?
What does it mean to me that I am a "tree planted by streams of water"?

NOW, draw or write what your winter season looks like. Is it soft and quiet? Bare but beautiful? Fierce and frozen with something stirring beneath?

Lastly, write this declaration:

I am not behind.
I am not broken.
I am not alone.
I am rooted in God's promises.
I am planted in love.
I am growing—right here, right now.

This season is not an end.

It is a beginning.

Listen to the silence. Listen within. Listen to nature. Listen for His voice. *It is in our stillness when we are able to hear clearly from our Lord.*

Reflection

_____

_____

_____

_____

_____

_____

_____

_____

_____

_____

＊ ＊ ＊

The seeds you have planted in obedience and love
　　will bloom in places you may never see —
　　but heaven will see, and heaven will celebrate.

Go, beloved gardener. Your work is ready for the Light.
　　Until we meet again in the garden,
　　keep blooming, beloved.

"He has made everything beautiful in its time."
~ Ecclesiastes 3:11

As you close these pages, know this:

Your garden is alive.
Your work is holy.
Your life is precious beyond words.
Tend your heart tenderly.
Prune what must be pruned.
Water your dreams faithfully.
Stand tall in storms.
And when it's time... bloom wildly,
with all the abandon of a woman who knows
she is loved.

The gates may close for now — but the Gardener is always near. He will meet you in every seed you plant, every prayer you whisper, and every dream you dare to believe in.

Final Garden Reflection

You are not the same woman who first picked up this book.

⚲ You have dug deep.

⚲ You have pulled weeds.

⚲ You have planted seeds.

⚲ You have allowed the Gardener of your life to touch the tender soil of your heart.

You have learned:

⚲ That winter has a purpose.

⚲ That pruning precedes blooming.

⚲ That droughts end in rain.

⚲ That your roots are growing deeper even when the surface looks barren.

YOU are flourishing.
You are a mighty oak.
An unbroken Cosmos.
A hidden garden of splendor.
You are a story still unfolding.
And the Gardener of your life isn't finished with
you yet.

As you come to the final pages:

→ Dream forward into new seasons — what will you plant next in your life?

→ Sketch, write, pray, plan — *whatever your heart needs.*

→ Let this space be an extension of your garden and your growth.

CLOSING THE GATES

As you gently close these garden gates, know that this is not an ending, but a beginning. The seeds you have planted here—the prayers, the dreams, the small brave steps, the quiet stillness, the deep-rooted faith—they are alive beneath the soil of your heart.

You may not yet see all the blooms, but the Gardener of your life is faithfully at work, watering, tending, nurturing each precious seed.

Some seasons will call you to be still.
Some seasons will stretch you toward the sun.
Some seasons will prune you tenderly.
Some seasons will call you to harvest and dance.

Wherever you find yourself, remember: You are never alone in the garden of life. God is with you — in every season, in every soil.

The garden gates may close for now, but the Gardener never leaves.

Keep watering your dreams with prayer.
Keep planting seeds of kindness.
Keep trusting the slow, sacred work of growth.
Keep blooming right where you are.

...And know that whenever you are ready, the gates of His heart — and this garden — will always swing wide open to welcome you.

Love Always,

Marya

This book was planted in my spiritual womb by my Heavenly Father — the Gardener of my soul.
Every seed, every bloom, every thorn... all for His glory.

To my family — who walk this garden journey with me:
Thank you for your love, your patience, and your grace.

To the women who pick up this book:
May you find yourself seen, loved, and rooted more deeply than ever before.
May you remember that your garden — your life — is precious, purposeful, and wildly beautiful in His eyes.

Thank you for letting me walk a few steps of your journey with you.

ABOUT THE AUTHOR

Marya Patrice Sherron, MFA is a writer, advocate, and community leader devoted to amplifying marginalized voices and building inclusive communities. A former professor of Creative Writing and Black Studies, Marya is the founder of KI Productions, an independent publishing and production company launched in 2021 with the guiding belief that *every story matters.*

As the author of four children's books—*Time to Dance, Small Big Gifts, Ruby's Big Swim,* and *What if My Pieces Don't Fit?*—Marya's storytelling has touched families across the country. Her work is honored in the Indianapolis Airport Sensory Rooms, offering representation and encouragement for individuals living with autism. She has also authored numerous guided journals, Bible studies, and self-help workbooks focused on growth, healing, and empowerment—especially for women navigating complex caregiving roles.

In 2024, Marya deepened her mission by launching *KI Productions' Neurodivergent Collection*—a platform dedicated to showcasing the voices of neurodivergent individuals and families. Through this collection of books, personal testimonies, and family resources, Marya continues to champion awareness, education, and lasting change toward a more inclusive world.

The filmmaking division of KI Productions is currently in development on a docu-series celebrating the global phenomenon of Live Reality Games and full-length documentary celebrating the life and legacy of Marya's late brother, James-Kious Kelly. These deeply personal projects reflect her commitment to storytelling that uplifts, educates, and inspires.

Beyond her creative work, Marya is a relentless advocate for families navigating disability. She facilitates *Caregiver Connection* through the Autism Society of Indiana and serves as the Program Coordinator for Ausome Indy's *Moms Mentoring Moms* program, creating vital support systems for parents of children with disabilities. She also lends her voice and leadership to several boards, including *The Arc Indiana* and the *Parks Foundation of Noblesville*, where she serves as *Inclusion Chair*, and is an active member of the *Women in Noblesville Committee*.

A champion of community-centered change, Marya also founded *Safe Parks Plus*, a safety-focused initiative advocating for fenced-in playgrounds to protect children who elope. Through policy work, storytelling, and service, she continues to build bridges of understanding, connection, and hope for families across Indiana and beyond.

Contact Marya: maryapatrice@gmail.com

Visit Marya's Shop: time2dance.org

facebook.com/kiproductions
instagram.com/KI.Productions928
linkedin.com/in/MaryaPatriceSherron

LOVE GROWS HERE

Let's Keep Digging...

Together.

Xoxo,
Marya

www.ingramcontent.com/pod-product-compliance
Lightning Source LLC
Chambersburg PA
CBHW061749120626
46550CB00005B/1940